From Pulpit to Public Square

"In *From Pulpit to Public Square*, Richard Voelz has crafted an essential guide for clergy navigating the sacred and transformative space between Jesus and justice, pulpits and the public square. In a world that desperately needs the power of faith in matters of fairness, equity, and compassion, Voelz offers clergy the tools and theological grounding to preach the good news of justice with integrity, authenticity, and purpose. He insists on the important truth that our faith traditions are not limited to the four walls of the church but extend to the highways and byways, the public squares, and the places where social transformation happens."

—LIZ THEOHARIS, Director of the Kairos Center for Religions, Rights, and Social Justice; cochair of the Poor People's Campaign; and author of *We Pray Freedom: Liturgies and Rituals from the Freedom Church of the Poor* and *We Cry Justice: Reading the Bible with the Poor People's Campaign*

"With a pastoral heart, a professor's precision, and a prophetic clarity, Voelz teaches like no other how to move from preaching in a pulpit to effective public proclamation—theologically, rhetorically, contextually, and strategically. He invites us into his faith-rooted classroom with honesty and hope so that we might learn more clearly what it means to have the skills and courage to speak and do justice, love kindness, and walk humbly with God in the public square."

—LUKE A. POWERY, Dean, Duke University Chapel, and Professor of Homiletics and African and African American Studies, Duke Divinity School, Duke University

"*From Pulpit to Public Square* is an invaluable resource for proclaimers interested in sharing the disruptive, world-changing gospel with the public. For those who believe 'God so loved the world,' Voelz has written a text that helps us communicate love beyond the walls of the church so that there will be both a hearing and an unsettling of the powers. A much-needed and deeply researched text, *From Pulpit to Public Square* offers a theologically grounded, deeply practical, and unashamedly prophetic training for public proclamation."

—TIMOTHY ADKINS-JONES, Pastor, Bethany Baptist Church, Newark, New Jersey, and Assistant Professor of Homiletics, Union Theological Seminary

"There has never been a time when the moral and ethical voice of the preacher is needed more in the public square. Voelz's excellent and timely book provides theological grounding, practical steps, and inspiring examples to equip and motivate preachers for engaging social issues in their communities. Whether speaking at a rally, city council meeting, press conference, or other civic event, preachers would do well to read *From Pulpit to Public Square* in preparation for this important form of public proclamation."

—LEAH D. SCHADE, Associate Professor of Preaching and Worship, Lexington Theological Seminary, and author of *Preaching and Social Issues*

"*From Pulpit to Public Square* invites us into an expanding conversation about the role and potential of Christian proclamation within society. Voelz thoughtfully explores homiletic methods, theologies, and theories relevant to both hesitant and seasoned preachers alike. This volume encourages courageous readers to connect daily wisdom, ethical commitments, and lived witness in practical ways that profoundly impact our collective well-being—here and now."

—LISA L. THOMPSON, Associate Professor and Cornelius Vanderbilt Chair in Black Homiletics and Liturgics, Vanderbilt University

"Voelz believes in a God as active in the public square as in a Sunday-morning sanctuary. With characteristic humility and hope, Voelz leverages his gifts as a teacher and preacher to equip faith leaders to make their witness accessible and relevant to the public work of justice. To his credit, he does not give simplistic, one-size-fits-all advice. He presses preachers toward questions of depth and conviction, and he provides concrete strategies for collaboration, discernment, and public engagement. Filled with examples and practical tools, *From Pulpit to Public Square* forms preachers who are courageous and wise in proclaiming God's commitment to the vulnerable."

—JERUSHA MATSEN NEAL, Associate Professor of Homiletics, Duke Divinity School

"Voelz's book *From Pulpit to Public Square* is an important contribution to redefining social justice advocacy as a witness to one's faith. Clergy engaged in advocacy often have to publicly justify their actions to critical onlookers. He has provided a valuable resource to justify advocacy in the public square as he connects it to one's faith by a theology of proclamation. His is a practical guide on standing for justice and understanding it as a component of Christian discipleship."

—JIMMIE R. HAWKINS, Presbyterian Church (U.S.A.) Director of Advocacy, Washington Office of Public Witness and Presbyterian Ministry at the United Nations, and author of *Unbroken and Unbowed: A History of Black Protest in America* and *The Shaping of Black Identities: Redefining the Generations through the Legacy of Race and Culture*

From Pulpit to Public Square

Faithful Speech beyond Church Walls

Richard W. Voelz

© 2025 Richard W. Voelz

First edition
Published by Westminster John Knox Press
Louisville, Kentucky

25 26 27 28 29 30 31 32 33 34—10 9 8 7 6 5 4 3 2 1

All rights reserved. No part of this book may be reproduced or transmitted in any form or by any means, electronic or mechanical, including photocopying, recording, or by any information storage or retrieval system, without permission in writing from the publisher. For information, address Westminster John Knox Press, 100 Witherspoon Street, Louisville, Kentucky 40202-1396. Or contact us online at www.wjkbooks.com.

Quotations from Miriam Y. Perkins, "The Praxis of Prophetic Voice: Martin Luther King, Jr. and Strategies for Resistance," *Black Theology* 17, no. 3 (November 17, 2019): 241–57. Used by permission of Taylor and Francis Ltd., http://www.tandfonline.com.

Book design by Drew Stevens
Cover design by Kevin van der Leek

Library of Congress Cataloging-in-Publication Data is on file
at the Library of Congress, Washington, DC.

ISBN: 978-0-664-26898-5 (paperback)
ISBN: 978-1-646-98437-4 (ebook)

Most Westminster John Knox Press books are available at special quantity discounts when purchased in bulk by corporations, organizations, and special-interest groups. For more information, please e-mail SpecialSales@wjkbooks.com.

*For those who hunger and thirst for righteousness,
whose vision of the world is shaped by God's realm,
and who dare to raise their voices beyond the sanctuary*

Contents

Acknowledgments	ix
Introduction: Public Proclamation: Moving Out of the Pulpit and into the Public Square	1
1. Theologies for Public Proclamation	19
2. The Self in Public Proclamation: Place and Power	35
3. Understanding the Contexts and Strategic Goals of Public Proclamation	55
4. Knowing What to Speak in the Public Square	79
5. The Shape of Public Proclamation: Form and Design	97
6. Dynamic Public Proclamation: Concretizing Devices, Lively Language, and Embodiment	113
Conclusion: Migratory Speech for Contenious Times and a Blessing for the Work	133
Appendixes	
Figure 1: Public Context Worksheet: Wide View	139
Figure 2: Public Context Worksheet: Close View	140
Figure 3: Strategic Goals Worksheet	141
Bibliography	143
Index	149

Acknowledgments

As this is a book on what I call public proclamation, I want to start by thanking those of you who dare to speak in the public square out of the depths of a faith that is committed to justice, love, truth, and openheartedness. Among you are full-time pastors, bivocational clergy, community organizers, chaplains, politicians, and committed laypeople. Whether we have met or not and whether you are widely known or known only in your community, you have inspired this book in so many ways. I hope that you see some of the marks of your labor in these pages, that it resonates with and affirms your work, and that it encourages you as you continue to speak in the public square. In particular, I want to name the leaders and fellow participants of RISC (Richmonders Involved to Strengthen our Communities) as a significant inspiration for this work. I also thank my dear friends and co-laborers in Milligan for All and want to name Jess Carter, one of our cofounders who passed away in 2024. The work we do together is inspiring, and as you will see throughout the book, I draw deeply from these efforts.

I must thank my students who have wrestled with and experimented with pieces of this material. To those of you who have taken the courses Proclaiming Justice in the Church and Public Square and Introduction to Preaching and Public Proclamation, I extend my deepest thanks. You have been thoughtful and creative in thinking about what public proclamation can be, and you have had the courage to raise your voices in our work together. There are too many of you to name here, but I think you will see many of our conversations and your questions, challenges, and ideas in these pages. Thanks for helping me to recognize what was helpful and what needed to be in this book for the sake of others.

I am privileged to have served on the faculty of Union Presbyterian Seminary since 2016, during a time in which so much in our world, the church, and theological education have changed. President Jacq Lapsley and Academic Dean Ken McFayden maintain a faculty culture prioritizing scholarship that "prepares people to be leaders of gospel-inspired transformative change in pursuit of a more just and compassionate world."[1] I hope that this book complements the seminary's mission to do just that. The staff at Union's world-class William Smith Morton Library was incredibly helpful in locating resources for me, especially Mengistu Lemma and Lisa Janes. I am grateful for the faculty colleagues who gather regularly across our two campuses for writing retreats to hold each other accountable and celebrate our writing. Thanks especially to Rachel Baard, who coordinates these times, and to Christian, Dorothee, James, Josh, Lakisha, and Rubén, who have been cheerleaders in our parallel writing times. Mike Frontiero, who formerly served as the seminary's communications director, comes to my class each year to work with students on media relations. These sessions have also shaped this book. I have completed the book on a sabbatical leave, and I am grateful that the seminary's board of trustees continues this generous practice.

My colleagues across the country and world in the Academy of Homiletics are a continuing source of inspiration and collegiality. I am thankful for the supportive relationships and environment that stimulate new work in preaching and beyond. You have provided many foundations for this book. I am a proud graduate of Vanderbilt University's doctoral program in homiletics and liturgics. The School of the Prophets has had a large hand in shaping my identity and in thinking about the ways that preaching is an important part of a broader world of theological communication. I am ever grateful for my time at Vanderbilt, for my doctoral mentors, and for my #VandyHandL kindred who support one another at every turn.

My faculty colleague Josh Morris read drafts of this book and generously offered comments. Additionally, Josh has used some of this material with his class on Union's Charlotte campus. Gail Davidson and Kristin Peters read the manuscript from their perspectives as congregational pastors, chaplains, and community organizers. These colleagues' insightful feedback has made the book better.

I dared to write this book only because Bridgett Green at Westminster John Knox Press took the time for a generative conversation about my teaching and writing. She helped me see the possibility for the book and encouraged me to follow it. David Dobson provided helpful guidance at the outset of this project. Stacy Davis carefully shepherded the manuscript,

---

1. "Mission & Vision," Union Presbyterian Seminary, accessed January 15, 2025, https://www.upsem.edu/about/mission-vision/.

and I am grateful for her insights and diligent work in editing the book. Thanks to the entire team at WJK who helped bring this book to reality.

My spouse, Meredith, and daughter, Elly, are sources of joy and energy, and their love grounds me. Thank you both.

I write at the dawn of a new presidential administration (one that triggered a great deal of distress in its first term), amid global conflict, and while we watch a planet literally burning. I am not naive about the challenges of our world right now and the enormity of the work for change before us. However, I am committed to the hope that I find in the story of God's continually unfolding, boundary-crossing, justice-making love. As a homiletician, it will come as no surprise that I think our words still matter. Let me say that again: Our words still matter. Thanks to each of you who have picked up this book, who will interact with it, and who will put these ideas into practice. I hope that what you find in these pages encourages and equips you to be part of God's story with your words beyond the pulpit and out in the public square.

Martin Luther King Jr. Day
Season after the Epiphany, 2025

Introduction

Public Proclamation
Moving Out of the Pulpit and into the Public Square

THREE IMAGES OF THE PUBLIC PROCLAIMER

When I introduce the term "public proclamation," at least three images come up in our popular imagination. First in many people's minds is the image of the street preacher, the person we typically find to be slightly askew, who occupies a very public space and offers very few words of hope but plenty of fire-branded, Scripture-laced condemnation for the vices of the world, overlaid with calls to repentance and naming the unpredictable return and subsequent judgment of Jesus. Growing up on the edge of NC State University in Raleigh, North Carolina, and spending plenty of time on campus as a young person, I became somewhat familiar with the ways of the person who was dubbed "the Brickyard Preacher." The Brickyard is a brick-laden space on campus where many students passed through on their way to classes. The preacher would stand with signs and Bible in hand, eager to blanket anyone who came near with their message of the day. Such preachers continue there and in many similar spaces today.[1]

These preachers are often at the center of controversy around free speech practices on college campuses and in civic spaces, not to mention the street corners for which they are so popular. Various issues emerge when we

---

1. Avery Davis, "NC State 'Brickyard Preachers' Cause Frustration, Questions among Students, Staff on Campus," *Technician*, October 18, 2021, https://www.technicianonline.com/news/nc-state-brickyard-preachers-cause-frustration-questions-among-students-staff-on-campus/article_d531f7d2-2fde-11ec-86bc-6f2c5c095840.html.

think about the street preacher, but they tend to revolve around a central question: Does this kind of speech belong in public spaces, and if so, what are its limits? Although Stanley Saunders and Charles Campbell have sought to rehabilitate and reclaim street preaching for those of us who are rightly skittish around this practice, many of us continue with the haunting image in our minds because of our encounters as observers or those who have received the sting of that type of preaching.[2]

The second image of public proclamation is more immediately present in our current political climate. This image is of the Christian pastor or politician (both typically identifying as male, cis-gender, heterosexual, and white) who publicly prioritizes faith as part of their political agenda and who takes to public rallies (often election-related), television news programs, and social media with a faith weaponized by white Christian nationalism, holding up so-called family values and using faith language to rail against LGBTQIA+ rights, reproductive rights, protections for immigrants, gun control efforts, and more. Recently, pastors like Robert Jeffries and others have made public appearances and turned their congregations into public platforms in support of the forty-fifth president's election and reelection campaigns. Other public leaders, such as former US military general Michael Flynn, have come into the public square through events like his ReAwaken America Tour, speaking faith language intertwined with a white Christian nationalist message.[3] These speakers twist Scripture and Christian theology to demean people groups, argue for harmful public policies that harken back to the Jim Crow era, and prop up authoritarian leadership in government. The rhetoric of these speakers comes across as caustic, adversarial, and, to one degree or another, constructing a worldview at odds with democratic principles and more generous constructions of Christian faith.

A third image is related to the second but strikes us as much more palatable. The charismatic faith leader steps forward in the midst of a protest, mass meeting, or during a press conference, responding to a tragedy or social injustice that has occurred. Their work is to galvanize and energize a crowd that comes from many faiths and no faith tradition whatsoever. They have gathered to respond to whatever the latest crisis in

---

2. Stanley P. Saunders and Charles L. Campbell, *The Word on the Street: Performing the Scriptures in the Urban Context* (Wipf and Stock, 2006).

3. Beau Underwood and Brian Kaylor, "The Sermon Michael Flynn Hopes You'll Hear," *Word&Way* (blog), July 14, 2022, https://wordandway.org/2022/07/14/the-sermon-michael-flynn-hopes-youll-hear/.

the community or nation happens to be. They stand shoulder to shoulder with an assortment of people: politicians, national organizers, and other faith leaders. A word is needed that can move the crowd toward solidarity, empathy, and action. So much hangs on this moment, and the charismatic faith leader opens their lips to speak with energy, power, and rhetorical flourish. The crowd cheers and participates at all the right places. They are captivated by the seemingly effortless words delivered with no (or very few) notes. Figures like Martin Luther King Jr., Jesse Jackson, Al Sharpton, William J. Barber II, and others quickly come to mind. And rightly so, given the roles that they have played in the overlap of US Christianity (or, perhaps more precisely, the Black church) and democracy.

Still, even if this image is more palatable than the street preacher or the white Christian nationalist pastor/politician and even if we find ourselves in full agreement with the content and the methods of the third image, not every faith leader can imagine themselves in that scenario. Few of us will step onto a dais in a public setting with crowds and cameras surrounding us, ready to offer a word that speaks to the masses on some momentous occasion in the nation or in the communities where we work, live, and seek to make a difference. When this third image of public proclamation arises, it might seem intimidating and out of reach for us. Even if we might imagine ourselves as having something to say in those moments, we frame those speakers and those moments as *Not for me!* We have trouble imagining ourselves in that role.

The problems with these images of public proclamation are twofold. In the case of the street preacher and the white Christian nationalist pastor/politician, we question not only their motivations but also their methods. Public proclamation for the street preacher moves the pulpit into the public square for a crowd who does not share the same assumptions or the same faith language and does not willingly gather for a word that not only feels antagonistic but actively harmful, not to mention archaic. For the white Christian nationalist pastor/politician, faith language is weaponized for authoritarian purposes that are harmful to individuals and groups of people and for the work of a healthy democracy.

In the case of the charismatic faith leader, we do not question their motivations. Often, we share their impulse to address the prophetic and pastoral needs of the moment—and we admire their methods. In the latter image, however, public proclamation often feels distant, uninhabitable, and much too large, perhaps like trying on an oversized garment. When I show videos of these occasions in class, students remark to me that these moments feel "too big" and unimaginable for their own vocational work.[4] While King's speech at the March on Washington in 1963 and William J. Barber II's speech before the Democratic National Convention in 2016 (two of such examples I have shown over the years) are iconic moments, and there is so much to admire in them, my students have difficulty imagining themselves occupying those spaces and those moments in the vocations and communities that lie before them. With these three images in mind, public proclamation either feels too foreign or too distant to make much sense as viable options for many (or most) of us.

A PUBLIC SQUARE, A PUBLIC GOSPEL

This book seeks to chart a way forward that helps public proclamation become something within our reach—whether we find ourselves on the big stage or, more likely, in those smaller, more humble platforms in the path of our various ministries. Whether you are a student preparing for a Christian ministry within traditional clergy roles or outside the church, a chaplain who moves in and out of public spaces, a nonprofit leader, or an experienced clergyperson looking for a resource to help you move faithful speech out of the sanctuary and into the public square, this book is designed to support you as you engage in the work of public proclamation, wherever that might happen.

I am a professor and scholar of preaching, and I spend much of my time with students who are preparing for a wide range of ministries. I have a responsibility to students preparing for congregational ministries as well as students who will never step into pulpits. These days, fewer and fewer students in the institution where I teach want to go into congregational ministry. The students who are committed to congregational ministries rarely see their roles as limited to the congregation. They see their ministries intersecting with what is happening in the public square. Rather than lament the reality of a decreasing number of people to train for traditional preaching ministries, I have shifted the way that I teach preaching, spending a few weeks of my introductory preaching course talking specifically about the work of public proclamation

---

4. For a more in-depth analysis from the perspectives of Black religious leadership, see Kyle E. Brooks, *Chasing Ghosts: The Politics of Black Religious Leadership* (Georgetown University Press, forthcoming).

and emphasizing what are often called "transferable skills."[5] One of this book's claims is that much of what we teach and learn about preaching can be adapted for the work of public proclamation.

Our current context requires our attention to the demands for public proclamation. When we consider the ongoing terrors that unfold in our communities and across our nation and world, faith leaders are anxious to offer a word to the public that meets the moment. Faith leaders bring a hunger to participate in the healing and flourishing of all people, beyond the walls of their congregations. Our media-saturated culture presents an immediacy to the needs of our community, nation, and world. In response, faith leaders are increasingly engaging in community and organizing efforts for housing, education, racial justice, LGBTQIA+ rights, women's rights, climate justice, gun control, and more. They are called to represent families and neighborhoods and as representatives of Christian faith when natural disasters strike or when other acute community needs arise.

But these occasions are not limited to emergency situations. Faith leaders serve nonprofits that seek to garner community support and financial backing for food insecurity, domestic violence response, racial reconciliation efforts, individuals with special needs, and many other ongoing service needs, as well as community justice efforts. They also show up regularly to speak and pray at city council meetings, school board meetings, and state legislative sessions.

In such work, we faith leaders are tasked not only with describing and interpreting what has happened or is happening and the needs of the population on whose behalf we are speaking but also naming a public gospel that forms the basis for hopeful action. Of course, we do so alongside, and on behalf of, leaders of other faith traditions and people with no faith commitments. When I say "public gospel," I do not mean *the* Christian gospel. Ed Farley makes a crucial distinction between "the gospel" and "Gospel." Rather than strictly limited to content or "verbal formulas" about Jesus Christ (the gospel), Gospel for Farley is "the mystery of God's salvific working. . . . It is something to be proclaimed, but the summons to proclaim it is a summons to struggle with the mystery of God's salvific action and how that transforms the

---

5. I hope that the book is clear that there is much more to public proclamation than just transferable skills, but rather a vibrant conversation about homiletical theories and practices moving back and forth across ecclesial and public spaces.

world. . . . Gospel is—and this is its prophetic element—disruption, an exposure of corporate oppression and individual collusion, and, at the same time, an uncovering of redemptive possibilities."[6] So when I suggest that we articulate a public gospel, we are not laying out in public spaces our doctrinal commitments concerning Jesus of Nazareth. Rather, we are aiming to say something disruptive that often points toward critique of the way things are. Even more, we seek to articulate redemptive possibilities for our common life together that are grounded in our belief that God is at work transforming the world.

The bottom line is this: Faith leaders do not drop their faith commitments at the door. Yet when we are called on to speak publicly, we cannot and do not do so in ways that fully approximate the kind of speaking we do within church walls and, more specifically, in the act of preaching a sermon in the context of Christian worship. As such, each faith leader who enters into the task of public proclamation must carefully consider what we will say and how we will show up, well before we are ever called on to do so. This book is for anyone searching for ways to faithfully speak a public gospel in the public square.

"PUBLIC" AND "PROCLAMATION": DEFINING TERMS

I have used the term "public proclamation" and have offered images that enter our minds, but I have yet to offer a more specific definition of that term. The "public" part of that is easiest to explain. By that, I simply want to differentiate between the kind of communication that faith leaders undertake within, and for the purposes of, Christian worship gatherings, and that which happens beyond them. As some conversation partners are quick to point out, Christian worship is public, and we have far too often kept those distinctions intact to the detriment of all.[7] I do not disagree with the aversion to the distinction, nor the critique. At a basic level, the failure of the distinction has become true even more so in light of how the COVID-19 pandemic propelled most US congregations into digital

---

6. Edward Farley, *Practicing Gospel: Unconventional Thoughts on the Church's Ministry* (Westminster John Knox, 2003), 81.

7. I credit local Richmond activist and faith leader Allan Chipman with offering this feedback in a conversation, as opposed to my own emphasis on the nonliturgical aspect of public proclamation. See also the work of Cláudio Carvalhaes as it relates to worship and public witness in Sebastian Kim and Katie Day, eds., *A Companion to Public Theology* (Brill, 2017); Rubén Rosario Rodríguez, ed., *T&T Clark Handbook of Political Theology* (Bloomsbury, 2019).

gatherings easily accessible to anyone who might tune in. When I use the term "public" as a modifier here, I am trying to suggest that faith leaders are communicating beyond the physical borders, constituted gatherings, and communicative expectations of regular Christian worship, especially via the genre we have come to know as the sermon or homily. Instead, faith leaders are communicating with and for audiences that inhabit the geographies and architectures of public spaces, for audiences that are often mixed with respect to their types of faith commitments, and for purposes different than Christian worship.

"Proclamation" requires more effort. This word comes to us from Latin roots, *pro*, meaning "before," and *clamare*, meaning "to cry out." In its noun and verb forms, it has crossed civic and homiletical lines through the years. In the civic arena, it has meant an official or formal public announcement. There is a sense of authority here, since a proclamation (or "to proclaim") would come via someone empowered to do so on behalf of an individual, group, or institution. Here we might think of decrees, laws, or special messages originating from civic authorities. Consider Abraham Lincoln's Emancipation Proclamation or a government official's call for the observance of a special day, week, or month on the calendar—such as Transgender Day of Visibility, Memorial Day, or Black History Month—or, on a smaller scale, a day in honor of a respected person in a local community. In this latter sense, proclamations serve communities by raising awareness, giving honor, and setting aside time and resources for special purposes.

When it comes to homiletics, the difficulty increases. As David Buttrick indicates, "Sometimes the term 'proclamation' is regarded as a fancy synonym for preaching. Indeed, in the Greek of the Christian scriptures, *kerysso*, 'to proclaim' or 'to herald,' is often used interchangeably with *euangelizo* 'to preach.' But the noun *kerygma*, 'proclamation,' has taken on special significance in the twentieth century."[8] With regard to this "special significance," Buttrick points to the work of early-twentieth-century scholar C. H. Dodd, who sought to differentiate between two terms. First is *kerygma*, or that which was preached or announced in the New Testament regarding Jesus in early Christian communities. Second, *didache*, the instruction and exhortation that was given to communities that had aligned themselves with the Jesus movement. Buttrick notes the effects that this has had on preaching in that "preachers were called to be 'kerygmatic'; they were 'heralds' who should deliver the same message that

---

8. David Buttrick, "Proclamation," in William H. Willimon and Richard Lischer, eds., *Concise Encyclopedia of Preaching* (Westminster John Knox, 1995), 384.

apostles once declared. From the 1940s to the 1990s, scarcely a book on homiletics appeared that did not refer to Dodd's *The Apostolic Preaching* and the idea of a primitive kerygma."[9] Without getting sidetracked by the details of the arguments behind this distinction, Buttrick points to the difficulty of Dodd's kerygma-versus-didache argument and the problems of making too many categorical distinctions about the nature of Christian preaching.[10]

Ultimately, Buttrick underscores that "what the term *kerygma*, 'proclamation,' does is underscore the character of the gospel as news, good news of a new state of affairs in our world." He continues by integrating the civic dimension of proclamation and suggests, "So the word promotes the gospel as announcement of a radically new human situation inaugurated by God. The gospel is 'public' because it speaks of a new social order. It is 'official' because it is from God. It is 'formal' because it is of ultimate significance. In every age, preaching is proclamation."[11] Likewise, John McClure observes that, for Richard Jensen, "proclamation is an event. It is an announcement that interrupts human existence with a saving word."[12] This is the character of what I mean by proclamation, even as I want to be clear: I do not simply mean that the sermon moves outside the doors of the church and into public space. As with public gospel, when we seek to engage in public proclamation, we are seeking to communicate a new social order "inaugurated by God."

The way that the term "proclamation" has crossed civic and homiletical lines benefits our purposes here and forms one of the book's central commitments. We might consider that for the work of public proclamation, among faith leaders there is a well-considered fluidity to the kind of faith speech that moves out of Christian worship and into public spaces and, perhaps, back again. As previously stated, one of the tasks of this book is to point to the resonances between preaching and public proclamation and to determine how preaching practices might inform the work of public proclamation. With these two words more firmly in hand individually, I now offer a working definition of what they mean together.

---

9. Buttrick, 385.
10. For more, see also Richard William Voelz, *Preaching to Teach: Inspire People to Think and Act* (Abingdon, 2019), xxii–xxiv.
11. Buttrick, "Proclamation," 385.
12. John S. McClure, *Preaching Words: 144 Key Terms in Homiletics* (Westminster John Knox, 2007), 115.

"PUBLIC PROCLAMATION": A WORKING DEFINITION

I want to offer a working definition of what I mean when I say "public proclamation" for two reasons. First, this is a working definition because it continues to evolve for me. In conversation with others, my definition seems to be continually under revision. And as you interact with it, you may have elements that you would like to add, take away, or reword. In fact, I would encourage you to do so. Second, and related to the first, I offer a working definition because I often encounter definitions of one term or another related to preaching and immediately feel both the hubris of the definer and the limits of the definition. I recognize that my working definition emerges from my particular and limited perspectives, experiences, and identity as a white, cisgender, heterosexual man who is well educated and middle-class. With that in mind, I offer the following definition:

> Public proclamation is communication that is intended for the public sphere, grounded in hope, and employing faith-rooted language, with the purpose of working toward strategic goals of offering witness amid trouble, uniting in solidarity, and/or working toward justice and healing.

"Communication"

Let me analyze the elements of this definition individually. First is the idea of "communication." This is a broad term and intentionally so. While for the purposes of this book we are considering oral speech practices, public proclamation entails a variety of methods of communication. In my work with an advocacy group around LGBTQIA+ concerns, we deployed a number of communication modes as part of an overall communications strategy that included print and TV journalism, web presence and social media, billboards, physical presence or disruption (or both), interpersonal communication, and more. In ongoing efforts, coordinating those various modes of communication was absolutely critical. Public proclamation uses a wide range of communicative practices across the spectrum of media. Limiting our definition of public proclamation to verbal speech would be unwise, even as the focus of this book is on public speaking.

I have already mentioned above what I mean by "public," and that distinction remains for this definition. I alternately use "public square" and "public sphere," and for me, there are no functional distinctions.

Some readers may be familiar with a more technical usage of public sphere from the work of Jürgen Habermas, who says that it is

> a domain of our social life in which such a thing as public opinion can be formed. Access to the public sphere is open in principle to all citizens. A portion of the public sphere is constituted in every conversation in which private persons come together to form a public. . . . Citizens act as a public when they deal with matters of general interest without being subject to coercion.[13]

The use of "domain" here is an important concept, as it relates in parallel fashion to "square," pointing to specific kinds of spaces. Whereas Habermas's use of "domain" and the concept of the public sphere is much wider and more conceptual in thinking about society—not to mention more idealistic—we also want to think here about the real kinds of physical spaces in which we might speak and how they relate to the more conceptual thinking about the public sphere. To reiterate what I have already suggested, when I use the term "public sphere" or "public square" here, I do so to indicate a space outside regular Christian worship gatherings and typically beyond Christian worship spaces. I say typically, because we know, of course, that many gatherings where public proclamation happens also take place in houses of worship. For instance, I have gathered with the Poor People's Campaign, a nonsectarian group, in a Unitarian Universalist congregation. And we know that Martin Luther King Jr.'s "I've Been to the Mountaintop" speech was held in a church, like many gatherings in the civil rights era were, blurring the lines between church and public sphere in many ways.[14]

"Grounded in hope"

The first two elements of the definition have been functional delimitations of what is happening and where. My definition now moves to describing the quality of that communication. The first of these is that this communication is "grounded in hope." I resonate with what many

---

13; Jürgen Habermas, "The Public Sphere," in *Rethinking Popular Culture: Contemporary Perspectives in Cultural Studies*, ed. Chandra Mukerji and Michael Schudson (University of California Press, 1991), 398.

14; This dynamic was true and necessary for Black churches. Black congregations have historically served as communal spaces, but especially in the civil rights era, they functioned in ways that were relatively (but certainly not entirely) safe from violence and threats.

have said about what we generally refer to as "prophetic preaching."[15] That is to say, as those who exhibit faith in the God of Israel and Jesus of Nazareth, I move through this world with the hope that God is not yet done with the work of redeeming the world and that we participate in that hope with meaningful action in our public and private lives. Whether the situations in which we speak require a more prophetic voice or a more pastoral one or whether we favor a more holistic term like "prophetic care,"[16] we tether our speaking to the hope of God's intentions to restore and renew creation and to reconcile humanity to God and one another.

"Employing faith-rooted language"

Closely related is the next element of "employing faith-rooted language." Every faith leader needs to answer what this means for themselves, and many of us will articulate what this means in different ways. I am borrowing and adapting the idea of faith-rooted language from Alexia Salvatierra and Peter Heltzel's concept of "faith-rooted organizing." They define this as "shaped and guided in every way by faith principles and practices. Faith-rooted organizing is based on the belief that many aspects of spirituality, faith traditions, faith practices and faith communities can contribute in unique and powerful ways to the creation of just communities and societies."[17] Salvatierra and Heltzel make an important distinction between "faith-based" and "faith-rooted" organizing. While "faith-based organizers use the same basic assumptions and methodologies that would be employed when organizing any other sector of society," incorporating people of faith into "Alinsky-style organizing," faith-rooted organizing "dr[aws] on the deepest wells of the beliefs, values, disciplines and practices of the people of God."[18] Although Salvatierra and Heltzel are talking about differences in organizing strategy, I believe this distinction also makes

---

15. For an account of the role of hope in prophetic preaching, see Voelz, *Preaching to Teach*, 35–50.

16. Dale P. Andrews used this term. See Phillis Isabella Sheppard, Dawn Ottoni-Wilhelm, and Ron Allen, eds., *Preaching Prophetic Care: Building Bridges to Justice, Essays in Honor of Dale P. Andrews* (Pickwick, 2018).

17. Alexia Salvatierra and Peter Heltzel, *Faith-Rooted Organizing: Mobilizing the Church in Service to the World* (InterVarsity, 2013), 9.

18. Alinsky-style organizing refers to early twentieth-century community organizer Saul Alinsky and his secular model of organizing that many faith-based groups have adapted. Salvatierra and Hetzel are making a distinction about the point at which religious belief and practice become operational in community organizing strategy. Salvatierra and Heltzel, 9.

a difference when we consider public proclamation as well. How and to what degree faith language emerges in public speaking differs among faith leaders, but I do want to suggest that faith-rooted language indicates something different from the kind of public speech by a faith leader that puts the language of faith completely to the side or the kind of faith language deployed in a sermon.

"For the purpose of working toward strategic goals"

The definition next names "purpose." Moments of public proclamation have both an individual purpose, specific to whatever situational moment demands it, as well as a consistent purpose related to an organization, group of people, or community. This signals not only a situation and a relationship but also a rhetorical purpose or quality to the instance of public proclamation. These purposes will vary, and we work later in the book to identify some appropriate possibilities, but a few examples at this juncture would include "to energize," "to galvanize," "to show empathy," or "to mobilize."

Closely related to purpose is "working toward strategic goals." Well-considered public proclamation might begin as a reaction to something that has happened or is happening, but it does not stay there. The best instances of public proclamation are highly integrated with the strategic goals of the organization, group of people, or community on whose behalf we might speak, even when such public proclamations are more improvisational and reactive. Speakers should know what they seek to accomplish in the overall situation of their speaking and how their speaking forms one component of an overall communicative strategy for purposes beyond the moment in which they are speaking.

"Offering witness amid trouble, uniting in solidarity, and/or working toward justice and healing"

I identify three broad strategic purposes, which form a cluster of umbrella terms by which speakers might categorize their work of public proclamation. A speaker might work toward all three strategic purposes, a combination of two, or only one, depending on the situation and the speaker's role. These terms also serve as pathways for thinking about how instances of public proclamation integrate with an organization, group of people, or community's specific strategic goals.

The first is "offering witness amid trouble." The word "witness" here does a lot of work in that it signals a specific role for faith and faith leaders. Faith leaders stand as representatives of faith communities (whether local congregations, denominations, or denominationally related organizations, faith-based nonprofits, etc.) as well as the beliefs and practices of those faith communities. As a witness in the public square, faith leaders offer a presence that makes claims about who God is and what God desires for our communal life. Notice that I do not say "witness to." I hesitate to offer the "to" or complete the phrase too quickly in this definition because the specific nature of this witness will almost assuredly vary from situation to situation and among different theological commitments. After a natural disaster, a faith leader might speak in order to "witness to God's presence and the power of community in the face of unspeakable loss." In response to instances of racist voter suppression, a faith leader might speak in order to "witness to God's desire for equality." These examples briefly explain why I leave the "to ——" incomplete, though I would suggest that faith leaders contemplate how they fill in the blank for each situation. The other half of this phrase, "amid trouble," signals that something is amiss in the social fabric. While faith leaders might well speak out when things are going well or when there have been successes related to strategic goals (and thus in response to a trouble that has been or is being repaired), more often than not, a present crisis, tragedy, or ongoing need requires attention.

The second broad purpose is that of "uniting in solidarity."[19] In the public square, we cannot assume that all people who gather do so with the same perspectives, assumptions, or commitments, even if the gathering's purpose or cause is front and center. Nor can we assume that all people will be affected the same way. If there is more than one speaker, they usually come from different perspectives and social locations and may be a mixture of representatives such as political leaders, community leaders, organizers, and those affected by the situation, in addition to faith leaders. Moreover, in an era in which faith leaders are seen with suspicion in the public square—and the public sees the church as distant or disconnected

---

19. I have chosen "uniting in solidarity" over "standing in solidarity" out of ableist concerns for the latter phrase. See AIDS Foundation Chicago, "Style Guide," accessed January 14, 2025, https://www.aidschicago.org/style-guide/.

from many situations—listeners may wonder what, if anything, the faith community has to add. As such, one of the purposes of speaking in the public square might be to unite those gathered in solidarity across differences for the common strategic goals of the gathering, organization, group of people, or community. The choice of "solidarity" matters here because it indicates the fact that differences can and will remain, while people can feel strong ties that knit them together for working toward shared purposes.

The third broad purpose is "working toward justice and healing." Again, faith leaders encounter different situations, and even one situation might have different possibilities for the kind of work that is needed. For instance, a faith leader speaking out after a mass shooting in the community might feel the need to work toward the community's healing or they might call for the community and political leaders to come together to enact commonsense gun laws. A speaker might try to do both. The idea here is that faith leaders are attentive to the situation and the strategic goals of the organization, group of people, or community in a way that holds open the possibility of offering what we have traditionally called "prophetic" and "pastoral" words.

I have also included this wording in particular because of how dismissive people can often be of public speeches as "just words." Here I want to signal that speaking in public is an integral component of faith leaders' work toward justice and healing. I recognize that people are skeptical of clergy and other public figures when it comes to the relationship of words and action. That said, words continue to have power to move people to action. To take a negative example, we see how the words of political and white Christian nationalist leaders led to the January 6, 2021, attack on the US Capitol. Well-planned and timely words have the power to move people to take up the work of justice and healing.

Again, I would encourage you to play with the definition I have offered and to think deeply about the implications of each word and phrase. This definition is not perfect or permanent. In fact, it has changed over the years as I have reconsidered aspects of it. What resonates for you when you read it? What insights do you have borne of your own experiences that would lead you to add to, take away from, or otherwise revise the definition? What excites you? What gives you pause or raises your anxiety?

INTRODUCTION

SIX FUNDAMENTAL QUESTIONS

The chapters that follow emerge out of what I call six fundamental questions for those who are preparing to engage in public proclamation. Some of these questions are answered long before faith leaders are ever called on to speak in the public square. Some questions arise more closely to the speaking moment. Sometimes we have a long time to plan; at other times we do not. The first few questions offer the deeper well from which we might draw when we are called on to speak on short notice. In these chapters, we draw wisdom from the field of homiletics, which is the study of preparation and embodiment of sermons. As such, I hope to offer a more familiar conversation partner to those who have been trained in preaching but not in public proclamation. As I said earlier, I think homiletics has much to offer. I also integrate insights from other theological disciplines, rhetoric, and literature from community organizing. Along the way, I provide examples to help illustrate different concepts and practices.

Chapter 1 invites readers into developing a theology of public proclamation, answering the question: *When I engage in the work of public proclamation, what commitments fundamentally ground my doing so?* This question provides the foundation on which faith leaders will base their speaking. By this, I do not just mean general concepts of justice, God's love, or the like. Rather, drawing on the work of Kelly Brown Douglas, Willie James Jennings, my own work, and others, I identify core concepts that help piece together a theology of public proclamation, or what I call a "communicative public theology," which can support faith leaders in times when they are called on to speak on a moment's notice and to speak amid the arduous work over the long haul.

Chapter 2 recognizes the unique role of speaking as a faith leader and encourages faith leaders to reflect on the question *What is my place in the communicative situation?* Speakers should understand how their own role and power in the communicative situation operate. This is different in the public square than in congregations, where understandings and expectations of pastoral leadership are generally shared among clergy and laity. Those people in congregational leadership may even wonder to what extent they represent their faith communities in the public square. Ultimately, understanding our place in the public square means knowing when we have a great deal of moral authority by virtue of who we are and the situations we face. At other times, our authority is less, and a different approach is needed. Some situations call forth more adversarial positions, while others build coalitions and solidarity. I offer an analysis of varying approaches to public proclamation, depending on our place in the context, sense of authority, and perceived power in speaking situations.

In chapter 3, two questions emerge around understanding the context and the strategic goals of the organization, group of people, or community. *How do I understand what's going on here?* and *What is the strategic goal of the communicative situation?* The first question underscores the importance of both contextual and social analysis that sets the stage for public proclamation. While we might be familiar with congregational exegesis, those who speak also need to understand the systems and actors at work in their public speaking situations.

The second major question encourages speakers to articulate what they hope happens as a result of their speaking, especially as it relates to the larger strategic goals of the movement or organization, group of people, or community for which they speak. In chapter 3, we explore tools for analyzing context and consider small- and large-scale goals as vital tools for preparing to speak.

The next three chapters deal more closely with discerning what to say and how to say it. In chapter 4, the fundamental question is *What are the theological emphases needed for this communicative situation, what do I want to say, and how do I hope people will respond?* When discerning what to say in the public square, faith leaders face a different situation than when in the pulpit. Understandings of Scripture and theology vary—as does their usefulness or applicability—depending on the context in which one speaks. And as chapter 3 indicates, faith leaders need to consider the manner in which they show up in the public square with their faith commitments.

In order to know what to say, faith leaders first need to articulate what "faith-rooted speech" means for them. Additionally, chapter 4 encourages us to be attentive to the kinds of theological questions that are emerging in the speaking situation in order to foster a faith-rooted response. Finally, recognizing some practices that cross over from sermon preparation, we consider how to formulate what is variously called a "core affirmation," "central claim," "focus statement," and other terms, as a way of being clear about what we are saying. As a corollary, we also formulate what is variously called a "central purpose," "behavioral purpose," or "function statement" as a way of articulating a particular purpose for the communication event and how it connects with strategic goals.

Finally, chapters 5 and 6 consider the question *What kind of rhetorical-communicative strategy will best help achieve the goal or goals?* Here also are some crossovers from sermon preparation, especially in three areas. First, thinking about sermon form or design can help us formulate an overall design for a speech that accounts for the ways that the how of speaking can follow the what. Sermon form also plans for the experience of listening and connects that to the communicative goals. Matters of form and design take up chapter 5. Second, speakers need to think about ways to make their claims concrete. There are connections here with communication strategies from community organizing. Third, but certainly not least, speakers should consider the artistry of language, emotion, and embodiment of speaking. These are not ornamentation or rhetorical flourish for their own sake, nor for manipulative purposes, but are integral to communicational design and conveying passion and authenticity in the speaking moment. These final three matters are the focus of chapter 6.

To help readers personalize and extend each chapter, I have included prompts or exercises at the end of or within each chapter. Prompts are intended to spur reflection on readers' personal situations and beliefs. Exercises are intended to help readers begin the work of public proclamation or deepen reflection on public proclamation, depending on each reader's level of experience. These concluding sections may be helpful for classes or for small groups of faith leaders committed to reading the book together.

A FEW MORE PRELIMINARY WORDS

Whether you are deeply experienced or brand new to the work of public proclamation, whether you are supremely confident or whether you shake in your boots, whether you speak on a big stage or a small one, my hope is that by the time you have finished this book, you will have some insights and strategies that help ground you in the work of speaking up and speaking out in the public square.

Faith leaders are uniquely positioned to offer our voices in the communities where we find ourselves. Our world is in desperate need of faith leaders committed to offering both a word of resistance to systemic evil and faith-rooted hope for all that is going on in our world. Yet we do not do so just because we happen to be ordained or because we have some theological education. If you are reading this book and thinking about speaking out before showing up, then let me raise a caution flag right now—a caution that goes double for people who walk through the world with tremendous amounts of privilege, as I do. The right to speak in the public square is earned, not given. Showing up with humility and a spirit of collaborative community-building well before the speaking moment is part and parcel of any work in the public square, especially since this work is often intercultural and interspiritual. To do otherwise is to risk harming others.

Finally, a note about the place from which I write. I write this book with no small amount of trepidation. I am a former pastor and a current seminary professor. I do not have a long history of organizing, and you will not find me on the local news or YouTube or on one of those big stages I mentioned at the beginning of this introduction. Because of my social location, it is often better that I show up with a presence of solidarity, rather than with my mouth open.[20] For those who do not know me, I simply want to be honest about my experience. But as I mentioned earlier, I do have experience planning and enacting communication strategy in a grassroots LGBTQIA+ advocacy group as we built that organization from the ground up. And I do have experience as a preacher, as a homiletician, and as someone who pays close and careful attention to how the words spoken by many different people in the public square operate.

Ultimately, I care about helping shape those who take up the work of public proclamation, and I write with the deepest hopes that this book helps each of us contribute to a more just and loving world, because that is at the core of my faith.

---

20. When interfaith leaders here in Richmond, Virginia, in the summer of 2020 organized local protests against the Confederate monuments and police brutality, a picture of the large gathering hit the news. Not even a fringe of my clergy stole was in the frame. "Richmond Clergy Demand Police End Violent Response to Protests," VPM, June 30, 2020, https://www.vpm.org/news/2020-06-30/richmond-clergy-demand-police-end-violent-response-to-protests.

1
Theologies for Public Proclamation

I remember the first time in my role as a pastor I was invited to offer the opening prayer for a city council meeting. As someone who had not yet been publicly engaged in the life of the city where I served, but in which I did not live, all sorts of questions rose to the surface as I reflected on this seemingly small task. *What is my role in this space? How do I relate to those who are present? What does it mean to be invited into this space? In what sense do I carry the fullness of my faith in this pluralistic space? What do I pray for?* As a preacher, I knew my role in the sanctuary and would agree with Otis Moss III that I was about the work of the "creation of an alternative world and an alternative consciousness."[1] And likewise, with Moss, I knew my homiletical role for the church "seeks contextualization and artistic imagination, drawn from engagement with scripture and deep, abiding spirituality. The preacher uses all the tools at her disposal, working to understand context in light of the limited freedom and agency of an ancient people and communicating grand theological ideas of the gospel."[2] In fact, this was well-worn ground for me. But in *this* space? This civic space? Something was changing. I felt as if I were a fish out of water and as if these noble descriptions of preaching had little practical wisdom to offer as I reconsidered the convictions that

---

1. Otis Moss III, *Blue Note Preaching in a Post-Soul World: Finding Hope in an Age of Despair* (Westminster John Knox, 2015), 26.
2. Moss, 27.

would ground my presence and witness there. Of course, I recognize that praying before a city council meeting is not necessarily setting the world on fire on the National Mall, nor is a prayer the same thing as a speech. However, this is the sort of small beginnings that many of us have with the work of public proclamation.

This chapter seeks to explore the first of our fundamental questions for public proclamation: *When I engage in the work of public proclamation, what convictions fundamentally ground my doing so?* I need to remember those small beginnings and the feeling of dissonance about my identity because my suspicion is that many of us will or have had that kind of experience to varying degrees. Even for those who were reared and trained in traditions where clergy cross the boundaries often between pulpit and public sphere, there is still a need to negotiate the differences in space and a need to (re)assess who we are and what grounds us in our boundary crossing.

I am a firm believer that theology and practice dance together. Like many practical theologians have articulated through the years, the loop of action and reflection helps refine our practices and sharpen our theological commitments, at whatever point we start. When we clarify our theological convictions for entering a practice, we are able to stand—not rigidly—but more firmly in our purposes. As Raphael Warnock observes of both Dietrich Bonhoeffer and Martin Luther King Jr, "Their preaching and prophetic witness were linked by the substance and intentionality of their *theological thinking*, which, more than anything else, provided a working hermeneutic for interpreting texts and times, for evaluating Christian speech and moral action."[3] This is the case with public proclamation as well. When faith leaders shift their communication from the pulpit and the familiar confines of the church's common worship to the varied settings of the public sphere, there is not a one-to-one correspondence either in theology or practice. With so much on the line when faith leaders cross this threshold then, we need to start with defining our why for engaging in public proclamation.

---

3. Raphael G. Warnock, "Preaching and Prophetic Witness," in *Bonhoeffer and King: Their Legacies and Import for Christian Social Thought*, ed. Willis Jenkins and Jennifer M. McBride (Fortress, 2010), 151.

DEFINING PUBLIC THEOLOGY

Perhaps, before exploring the finer grain of theological commitments that might characterize our speaking, we should start with defining how public proclamation fits within what we might call "public theology." The still-emerging work of public theology is complex, raising important questions about what we might mean about both "public" and "theology." To be sure, as a focus of theology writ large, there is plenty to be said. And there are many entry points for articulating a particular vantage point for how one does or makes a case for public theology.

E. Harold Breitenberg provides some initial definitions of what we might mean when talking about public theology. First, Breitenberg notes that public theology "is theologically informed discourse that seeks to be understandable both to those within its own religious tradition and to those outside it."[4] Here we see something of the character of what I mean when defining "public proclamation." The person speaking seeks to do so as one "theologically informed," but for those within and beyond their religious tradition. Jennifer McBride describes this situation when an Episcopal priest named Tim Clayton comes to the microphone to speak about the Iraq War during a people's town meeting in 2006 at the University of Southern Maine. McBride records Clayton's words that day:

> As a Christian priest, as a Christian pastor, I felt compelled to come tonight to bear witness to the witness of Christian scriptures relative to these issues. Christian ideas and pieces of the bible have been used so much in all this—particularly during the build-up to the war in Iraq, in an attempt to justify it—that I simply feel I must speak to give testimony to what the witness of the Christian scriptures is if we read it as a whole and let it speak to us with integrity and do not pick out the pieces and do not approach it trying to justify an end upon which we have already decided.[5]

Clayton seeks to offer a theologically informed position for a broad audience.

---

4. E. Harold Breitenberg Jr., "What Is Public Theology?" in *Public Theology for a Global Society: Essays in Honor of Max Stackhouse,* ed. Deirdre King Hainsworth and Scott R. Paeth (Eerdmans, 2009), 4.

5. Jennifer McBride, *The Church for the World: A Theology of Public Witness* (repr., Oxford University Press, 2014), 3.

Significantly the Episcopal priest is offering his position on a specific and important issue: the Iraq War. This points to Breitenberg's second definition of public theology as

> concerned with issues, institutions, interactions, and processes that are of importance and pertinence both to the church or other religious communities and to the larger society, including those of the same religious traditions, those of other faiths, and those who claim no religious beliefs and maintain no formal religious ties. Public theology interprets public life, engages society and its institutions, and offers guidance to and for society and its different sectors, interactions, and organizations.[6]

Here, Breitenberg's definition points us to the subject matter to which public theology attends. For Clayton's speech, we see that the Iraq War is something that crosses boundaries of concern. The church and public square are both concerned about the war-making efforts of the United States, and Clayton seeks to speak in a way that attends to its particularity as an ecclesial concern while suggesting that his theological framework functions as a vital contributor and moral good for the wider society.

Breitenberg suggests a third dimension to public theology, in that it "draws on and makes use of sources of insight, terminology, and forms of discourse and argument that are in theory available and open to all, in addition to ones that are explicitly religious and specific to the religious tradition in which the public theology develops and from which it speaks."[7] Even in this snippet from Clayton's speech, we can see how he invokes the "Christian scriptures," which are, ostensibly, part of the sources of wider public life in the United States or, at the very least, are accessible to all for further engagement. We might distinguish this from Clayton quoting from, say, Augustine or a contemporary theologian, neither of whom would be highly recognizable or nearly as authoritative as the Christian Scriptures are in US public life and moral reasoning. This is to say nothing of the form of Clayton's discourse and argument, which McBride characterizes as in the mode of confession, in which "Christians have been in collusion with military might to the detriment of witnessing to Christ."[8] We explore further forms of discourse and argument in a

---

6. Breitenberg, "Public Theology," 5.
7. Breitenberg, 5.
8. McBride, *Church for the World*, 3.

later chapter, but it is sufficient to note here that the mode of confession is a form that the broader public recognizes and to which it is open, rather than a traditional, ecclesially known sermonic form.

This book is not a primer for public theology, so I do not go further into making distinctions about its nature and tasks, though they are certainly important. However, I do want to further characterize reflection on the work of public proclamation as what we might call "practical public theology"—a combination of practical theology and public theology—or "communicative public theology," which adds the modifier about the specific practice on which we are focused. In other words, our primary entry point to the work of public theology is from the vantage point of how public theology is "performed."[9]

For our purposes, then, public theology stands by its intentions in distinction to confessional theology or systematic theology.[10] Confessional theology serves the church in the form of ecclesial and liturgical bodies, a sort of internal communication providing references for its faith language and processes of meaning-making. Systematic theology likewise serves the church but does so through academic categories and discourse that are focused on clarifying doctrinal matters for the church (primarily) and for other interested (and perhaps public) partners.

Those of us who desire to speak faithfully in public enter the work of public theology through a communicational lens. I recognize that the entry point of communication is not sufficiently theological for some, at least in traditional terms and at first glance. In contrast, I want to suggest that this entry point *does* indicate a possible theological starting place for those of us who are moving from pulpit to public square. To be clear, I am pointing to a sense of the incarnated *logos*, Jesus of Nazareth, as God's self-communication, an idea that comes to us from Karl Rahner.[11] This Jesus embodied in word and deed the good news of God's liberative love. In this sense, as we see later, Jesus' proclamation as an agent of God's intervention typifies and models a kind of framework for grounding communicative public theology, speaking into a range of publics within a broader contextual public sphere.

---

9. Katie Day and Sebastian Kim, "Introduction," in *A Companion to Public Theology*, ed. Sebastian Kim and Katie Day (Brill, 2017), 17.

10. Day and Kim, 15–16.

11. Paul D. Molnar, "God's Self-Communication in Christ: A Comparison of Thomas F Torrance and Karl Rahner," *Scottish Journal of Theology* 50, no. 3 (1997): 288–320.

THEOLOGICAL FRAMES FOR PUBLIC WITNESS

The remainder of this chapter is dedicated to exploring three options for theological frameworks of what I am calling communicative public theology. In no way are these exhaustive. And I am not necessarily interested in readers adopting my specific theological grounding, which I will explore below. Since my communicative public theology comes from a particular social location and theological perspective, it is unnecessary to universalize a theological perspective for grounding *all* communicative public theology.[12] In the following options, I hope that you are able to find resources to responsibly construct your own communicative public theology in a way that leads to mutual flourishing, the common good, or, if you will, salvation.

Willie James Jennings: A Christo-Contextual Approach

In a provocative essay, theologian Willie James Jennings suggests understanding public proclamation as "speaking gospel in public space from . . . the position of the slave." By this, Jennings means "seeing public life from the position of those caught in the most detrimental effects of the operations of the market, the military, and statecraft."[13] Jennings invites those who consider public proclamation to move, in a sense, on the ground of the enslaved. Moreover, Jennings suggests that because enslaved people are present in multiple places in public life, so too is the gospel that Jesus spoke. According to Jennings, "Wherever creatures are subjugated to the forces of death, there the gospel may and must reach, announcing the claim of God on creation—but it also characterizes a body extended across a vast terrain of need and suffering as when Jesus looked out onto the crowd and had compassion for them."[14] From here Jennings extends his outlook to the crowd that surrounded Jesus throughout the course of his ministry—a crowd that "presents public life as a state of emergency. . . . The body of the slave is mapped across the crowd. The crowd screams out to Jesus, and he shares in their screams. This

---

12. Jennifer McBride is helpful on this as she articulates her own understanding of public witness vis-à-vis Dietrich Bonhoeffer and dominant church communities. See McBride, *Church for the World*, 9–10.

13. Willie James Jennings, "Speaking Gospel in the Public Arena," in *Preaching Gospel: Essays in Honor of Richard Lischer*, ed. Charles L. Campbell et al. (Cascade Books, 2016), 188.

14. Jennings, 189.

gospel is fitted for this public, a crowd public."[15] Jennings's framework seeks to buttress a few reference points: the enslaved, the crowd, and Jesus. To these he adds a primary example in Martin Luther King Jr. The subjugated "crowd" was primary in King's speaking, as someone whose life included the real bodies of the enslaved in the US context and whose speaking emerged from and for those who are subjugated.

In this creative assemblage, Jennings not only roots the act of public speech in the person of Jesus but also suggests that the content of such speech is wide-ranging. King and those like him "spoke in ways that named the plight of black folks within their specific material conditions and deeply connected that plight with the will of the living God for their redemption and their liberation."[16] Thus, not only does public speech find justification in the person of Jesus, but those things that might be deemed "too political" by religious authorities are bound to God's own desire for the redemption and liberation of all people, but especially of those who live under threat.

At this point, we might be tempted to leave Jennings's elaboration of four characteristics for speaking gospel in public to our later chapter on communicative strategy. However, the characteristics Jennings describes are so thoroughly theological in nature that they warrant discussion here. Jennings's first category is that "speaking gospel in public is fragmentary speech," by which he means that biblical phrases, quotes, allusions, and stories find their way into public speech as "broken speech, piecemeal speech," which "follows the path of Jesus of being broken open in eucharistic form." Continuing to paint a christological-rhetorical picture, Jennings notes that these "gospel fragments flow from his broken body and find their way into such speech in ways that are not just rhetorical ornamentation but give shape to a verbal confrontation with powers arrayed to do harm."[17]

The second characteristic is that "speaking gospel in public demands we make connections." Here Jennings points to the ways that social problems are deeply intertwined with one another and work toward the harm of individuals and communities. Again, Jennings is not talking about a flat sociological analysis of social problems or even what we might call intersectional analysis. Instead, he grounds his thinking in God's own salvific action of "eagerly claiming creation, drawing all things to the divine life and inviting us to be messengers of this good news."[18]

15. Jennings, 190.
16. Jennings, 190.
17. Jennings, 191.
18. Jennings, 192.

Third, Jennings explains that "speaking gospel in public means uncovering those with power who are being influenced by the principalities and powers."[19] Yet again, Jennings demonstrates a Christocentric rhetoric suggesting that the one who speaks does so in the way of Jesus, inviting speakers to imitate "the prophetic sound of Jesus' voice as he unmasked the hypocrisy of the religious caste of Israel. . . . The issue is the naming of sin in and with the concrete actions of those with power."[20] This kind of speech is dangerous, since the principalities and powers inherently exercise power over, rather than power with, those who suffer. And it might strike us, in combination with the previous characteristic, as solely condemnatory and judgmental. At the same time, Jennings points to a fourth characteristic of "mak[ing] hope public." Jennings is careful to follow his own logic, not just naming hope in "temporal and linear dimensions" but also affirming that hope "has most decisively a spatial dimension and a communal character which is rooted in the incarnation itself. In Jesus, God lodges hope in the space of the creature and brings hope to the places of suffering, pain, and death."[21] To return to Jennings's beginning, just as the body of Jesus brings together the present concerns of suffering people (and for the enslaved), so too does public speech.

I have followed Jennings's argument at length in order to demonstrate how thoroughly theological his account of speaking gospel in the public arena extends. Were we to ask Jennings our first fundamental question (*When I engage in the work of public proclamation, what convictions fundamentally ground my doing so?*), Jennings would respond, as we have seen above, in a christological manner, yet with the historical inheritance and lens of the African American experience.

Kelly Brown Douglas: A Kairotic Theocentric Approach

Whereas Jennings's impulse for public proclamation runs through a christological and contextual lens (Christ via the enslaved), Kelly Brown Douglas grounds differently what she calls "prophetic black testimony."[22] Douglas suggests what I call a kairotic theocentric approach.

---

19. Jennings, 194. "Principalities and powers" is a reference to Eph. 6:12.
20. Jennings, 194.
21. Jennings, 195.
22. Kelly Brown Douglas, *Stand Your Ground: Black Bodies and the Justice of God* (Orbis Books, 2015), 207.

By this, I point to the way that she expresses the exigency of prophetic Black testimony. According to Douglas,

> This time in the life of the country is a *Kairos* time. *Kairos* time is the right or opportune time. It is a decisive moment in history that potentially has far-reaching impact. It is often a chaotic period, a time of crisis. However, it is through the chaos and crisis that God is fully present, disrupting things as they are and providing an opening to a new future—to God's future. *Kairos* time is, therefore, a time pregnant with infinite possibilities for new life. *Kairos* time is God's time. . . . It is God calling us to a new relationship with our very history and sense of self, and thus to a new relationship with one another, and even with God.[23]

As Douglas highlights figures like Martin Luther King Jr., she underscores Black prophetic testimony's role in holding the country accountable for its actions. This role extends from Douglas's sense of God's activity in the *kairos* moment and human cooperation with God's presence, disruption, and offering of a different future. To be clear, Douglas is not confining prophetic Black testimony to acts of public proclamation. She certainly has a wider view of speech and action in mind. For our purposes, we are focusing on how her sense of *kairos* might help theologically ground public proclamation.

This theological account manifests in four distinctive characteristics of prophetic Black testimony, particularly in that of King's speeches.[24] First, Douglas outlines what she calls "moral memory," which is "nothing less than telling the truth about the past and one's relationship to it. Moral memory is not about exonerating ourselves for the past. Rather, it is taking responsibility for it. To have a moral memory is to recognize the past we carry within us, the past we want to carry within us, and the past we need to make right."[25] While she does not elaborate on how her kairotic theology informs what she makes of moral memory, we do not need to press ourselves far to see how God's timely intervention gives to those who are attending to it a reading of the past, present, and future and their effects on real bodies, particularly those who have been subjugated in stand-your-ground culture. As she continues, she describes how moral memory "allows one to recognize how, in fact,

---

23. Douglas, 206.
24. Douglas does not name these. I am opting to call them "characteristics."
25. Douglas, 221.

the past is not past but continues to shape present realities."[26] God's kairotic intervention provides the characteristic contrast that allows memory to shed light on the past and present, then to respond by redirecting the future.

Douglas continues with the characteristic of "moral identity." Drawing on Paul Tillich and King, she suggests that "moral identity is one that is relieved of pretensions to superiority. It lets go of any myths that suggest one people is more valuable than another or that one people is chosen by God while another is not. . . . Essentially, it is with a moral identity—as King suggested—that one lives into the image of a God who is freedom."[27] While at first this seems like a departure from the kairotic, she also points to Jesus as both an exemplar and whose face we see in "the crucified class of one's own time" and "in the victims of a stand-your-ground-culture war."[28] It seems that Douglas's sense of kairotic inbreaking allows the possibility for reframing how we see and relate to the world around us (moral identity), as noted earlier.

Third, Douglas describes what she calls "moral participation," painting a picture of embodied participation in the struggle for "freedom, love, and life." According to Douglas, this is a matter of faith, which is more than assent to beliefs or doctrines, but rather active, embodied living that "is, therefore, reflecting the already/not-yet reality of God's kingdom. It is being the change that is God's heaven."[29] Again, the sense of *kairos* time comes to the fore, here linking prophetic testimony to prophetic action as a hallmark of public proclamation.

Fourth and finally, Douglas outlines the function of "moral imagination," which "is grounded in the absolute belief that the world can be better."[30] By this, Douglas suggests that the world Scripture imagines is not yet aligned with the world as it is. The moral imagination calls forth the belief that God is not yet done with the world and "disrupts the notion that the world as it is reflects God's intentions. With a moral imagination one is able to live proleptically, that is, as if the new heaven and new earth were already here."[31] Moral imagination is that which tethers the faith community to a hope-filled living, confident

---

26. Douglas, 222.
27. Douglas, 223.
28. Douglas, 223.
29. Douglas, 224.
30. Douglas, 225.
31. Douglas, 225.

that "God's universe does in fact bend toward justice."[32] Again, time is at stake here, recognizing God's role in time, as well as our own. I would be remiss if I did not mention that Douglas specifically highlights this as a dimension of Black faith, which inspired the prophetic testimony of King and many others.

A Theocentric Pattern of Transformative Intervention

Finally, I want to name my own theological grounding for public proclamation. While I am energized by elements of each of these prior accounts and do not see them as wholly incompatible, my own commitments are framed differently. In my book *Preaching to Teach*, I imagine preaching through the lens of critical pedagogy, which sees teaching as a public intervention that always has a vision of the public sphere in mind and which, according to Henry Giroux, seeks to "create the conditions that give students the opportunity to become citizens who have the knowledge and courage to struggle in order to make despair unconvincing and hope practical."[33] In the book, I narrate the convergences I see with preaching and critical pedagogy, but I am also careful to point out the theological grounding for the preacher as teacher. In this case, I draw from both homiletician David Buttrick and New Testament scholar Brian Blount in highlighting the critical importance of the *basileia tou Theou*, a Greek term in the Gospels that has variously been translated as the realm, reign, kingdom, empire, and even kin-dom of God.

Blount's understanding of the relationship between preaching the *basileia tou Theou* comes most clearly through the Gospel of Mark, by which "every narrative theme develops from the primary assertion that in Jesus Christ God has intervened into human history. That mythological reality is represented historically in the text by Jesus' assault against oppressive political, economic, and cultic boundaries."[34] In other words, Jesus acts as God's intervention in the world, a strategic representative of the power of the *basileia tou Theou*, and particularly through his preaching. But as Blount reads the Gospel of Mark, Jesus does not function alone in this role. In fact,

---

32. Douglas, 226.
33. Henry A. Giroux, *Teachers as Intellectuals: Toward a Critical Pedagogy of Learning* (Praeger, 1988), 128.
34. Brian K. Blount, *Go Preach! Mark's Kingdom Message and the Black Church Today* (Orbis Books, 1998), 82.

It is not, however, as an act/event unique to Jesus. His preaching is presented by Mark as both the successor to John's proclamation of God's intervention through him, and the prototype for the preaching of those who follow him as disciples. Their contemporary preaching in the Markan community is to do what Jesus' preaching did a generation before, establish the kingdom of God as a "pocket" that resists the oppressive social, religious and political boundaries that litter the landscape of human living.[35]

While this kind of proclamatory intervention has historically become more limited to preaching in common worship, we do well to remember that Jesus' proclamation was not limited to the confines of Jewish worship but took place in the public sphere as well. Living into the realm of God involves faithfully following the long line of those who have performed public interventions with an invitation to transformation. According to Blount, "The transformative kingdom power, resident in preaching, that Jesus wielded resides effectively now in the hands of his appointed disciples."[36] This is an important distinction: Those who follow Jesus are not just proclaiming Jesus, but rather the transformative power of the *basileia tou Theou*, and life lived in its shape. This is why, even though Jesus is a central figure, I call this a theocentric pattern of intervention. At the heart of proclamation is the radical imagination of the *basileia tou Theou*, the God who animates it, who summons us to proclaim its proximity, and calls us to follow in the chain of those who have sought to bring transformative intervention through the close relationship between speech and action.

A Pause on the Prophetic?

Readers will likely notice that I have not mentioned the prophets of the Hebrew Bible or "prophetic speech" as a theological grounding for public proclamation. This is intentional on my part. I recognize that William J. Barber II and Walter Brueggemann have helped many of us with their visions of the prophetic.[37] However, I am worried that the language of the "prophetic" has captured the collective attention

---

35. Blount, 83–84.
36. Blount, 94.
37. William J. Barber II and Barbara Zelter, *Forward Together: A Moral Message for the Nation* (Chalice, 2014); Walter Brueggemann and Davis Hankins, *The Prophetic Imagination*, 40th anniversary ed. (Fortress, 2018).

of many Christian clergy in ways that are pressurized, singular, and style-based and thus renders a model of both preaching and public proclamation that is ill-fitted for many of us. To put it plainly, being "prophetic" carries a lot of baggage in its content, approach, and the stylistic ways that our popular religious imagination has characterized prophetic proclamation.

According to David Schnasa Jacobsen, the long-lasting legacy of nineteenth-century Old Testament scholarship has affected the ways we approach preaching as prophetic. For Jacobsen, "The operative vision [of the prophet] is something akin to the Lone Ranger. As a prophetic preacher, one adopts a stance of disconnection with the hearers and tries to convince them of a need to adopt a universalizable liberal principle. . . . The prophet is the individual trying to reform the primitive system. Prophets are moral geniuses and religious innovators. They speak a word of individual insight in the hope of redeeming a corrupt social grouping."[38] What Jacobsen does not say is that in contemporary imaginations, the prophetic is also limited to the performance of masculinity.[39]

This Lone Ranger image haunts (to borrow the language of Kyle Brooks) current models of prophetic preaching and public proclamation, rendering a fairly singular image of what prophetic witness looks and sounds like. The conditions of the prophets and their relationships to power and community are different now from what they were in the ancient Near East, and as Jacobsen notes, the situations from which the prophets in the Hebrew Bible emerged were not uniform anyway. As it relates to preaching, Jacobsen advocates recognizing the multiple models of prophetic testimony as it develops elsewhere in the Hebrew Bible and acknowledging the prophetic discernment and proclamation that arises from communities in the New Testament. Preaching today, according to Jacobsen, should very much account for "encouragement" of the people and not simply "pulpit moralism."[40] I agree with Jacobsen's redirection for our notions of the prophetic. It is important to recognize the relationship between prophetic preaching and public proclamation in this regard. And though I know I am swimming against the tide by avoiding

---

38. David Schnasa Jacobsen, "Schola Prophetarum: Prophetic Preaching toward a Public, Prophetic Church," *Homiletic* 34, no. 1 (2009): 15.

39. See also the work on Kyle E. Brooks as it relates to the performance of Black charismatic religious leadership. "Ghostly Ideals: The Hauntology of Black Religious Leadership—Kyle E. Brooks, PhD," February 17, 2023, YouTube, https://www.youtube.com/watch?v=8RTxuQBQxPQ.

40. Jacobsen, "Schola Prophetarum," 20.

this terminology, I do hope that it makes a difference that I hold back from using it so that perhaps we can approach it with more nuance.

NOW WHAT?

In one of my classes, I share a video of Milton West, who appears on the *Today* show shortly after the town of Mayfield, Kentucky, was almost entirely leveled by tornadoes right before Christmas in 2021.[41] At that time, West was pastor of the First Christian Church (Disciples of Christ) in Mayfield, which was destroyed. Students are often just getting started with thinking about how to respond on their feet, in the moment, to questions that might come their way. In my estimation, West does a wonderful job of responding to and redirecting questions from the *Today* show interviewers. Students often marvel that he can do so amid tragedy and the pressurized moment of a nationally televised interview setting. I suggest that he is able to do this because he has considered the answer to our prompting question well before he gets to this moment. He has thought about his role as a public theologian and the work of practical/communicative public theology in such a way that it seems somewhat effortless on his part. My invitation is for us to do the same as a beginning point.

There are other grounding theological perspectives for how one understands public proclamation. Process theologians, for instance, might suggest that the pulpit is no different from the public square in that the impetus to speak, and the content of our speaking, is a response to God's "lure," "invitation," or "whispered Word" that is ever emerging in a changing world.[42] Womanist theologians might suggest a posture for public proclamation grounded in tenets of radical subjectivity, traditional communalism, critical engagement, and redemptive self-love with particular attention to Black women's speaking.[43] Those informed by Johann Baptist Metz might speak of

---

41. "Minister of Kentucky Church Talks Tornado Damage," December 13, 2021, YouTube, https://www.youtube.com/watch?v=P9B1DyB2lJs.

42. See, for instance, Ronald J. Allen, *You Never Step into the Same Pulpit Twice: Preaching from a Perspective of Process Theology* (Cascade Books, 2022); Marjorie Hewitt Suchocki, *The Whispered Word: A Theology of Preaching* (Chalice, 1999).

43. See, for instance, how Kimberly Johnson analyzes Black women's preaching through a rhetorical and womanist lens in Kimberly Johnson, *The Womanist Preacher: Proclaiming Womanist Rhetoric from the Pulpit* (Lexington Books, 2019).

the "dangerous memory of Jesus," which "holds a particular anticipation of the future as a future for the hopeless, the shattered and oppressed" and act accordingly.[44] I do not want to minimize any of these or other possibilities. We could go on from here, but at this point, it is important to reflect on how *you* answer the framing question of this chapter. What about your theological tradition and the theological well from which you draw ground you in having something to say in the public square?

EXERCISE YOUR VOICE

As I conclude this chapter and we turn to our next question, consider the following prompts as a way of answering the fundamental question of this chapter for yourself:

—What theological convictions help shape my point of view as someone who speaks?
—How and why does God care about what I feel compelled to speak?
—What does my faith say about this moment?
—What might this occasion or situation look like through the lens of radical imagination/hope? What do I hope will happen in the world, and how does that reflect my theological convictions?
—How am I connected to those in the situation? In what way does the church relate to the world through this speaking occasion?
—How is speaking a faithful response in the public square speaking for and with those in the situation?
—How does faith play a role in this communicative situation—even for those who do not believe the way I do?

---

44. Johann Baptist Metz, *Faith in History and Society: Toward a Practical Fundamental Theology* (PublishDrive, 2007), 89.

2
The Self in Public Proclamation
Place and Power

"The most common way people give up their power is by thinking they don't have any."

—Alice Walker[1]

TWO SPEECHES, TWO CONTEXTS

As we move toward thinking about the minister's public, communicative self, consider the two following vignettes:

1. On June 29, 2024, the Poor People's Campaign: A National Call for Moral Revival held a mass gathering in Washington, DC, in the shadow of the Capitol. Clergy across many Christian denominations and faith traditions, laypeople, community organizers, supporters, and interested observers gathered. The purpose of the meeting was to galvanize people in their support of the disenfranchised and to encourage voter outreach and center the concerns of "low wage infrequent voters ahead of the 2024 US elections and beyond."[2] Several minutes into the gathering, a choir took the stage clothed in T-shirts that said, "We are the swing vote." Together they sang a gospel- and hip-hop–inspired song with the refrain "Take back the mic and tell the truth." In front of the choir, someone held a sign that said, "We are a resurrection." As the choir finished and the members took their seats, William J. Barber II approached the microphone at center stage, clothed in a clergy collar and stole, and said,

---

1. This quote is widely attributed to Alice Walker but does not appear in her published work.
2. "The Mass Poor People's & Low-Wage Workers' Assembly & Moral March on Washington D.C. & to the Polls," June 29, 2024, YouTube, https://www.youtube.com/watch?v=Ilov3Qby5ws.

The last image that most Americans have of this Capitol behind us was a violent mob attacking it to undermine democracy. But we are gathered here today as a nonviolent army of love . . . and truth. We don't need to be an insurrection because we are a powerful resurrection. We are here today as America's—and representing America's largest potential swing vote: poor and low-wage brothers and sisters who make this country work, determined with our moral and religious labor [sic] social justice advocate allies. We are determined that it is time to rise up and say together: it is time to climb and take this nation to higher ground. And we stand in a long tradition, brothers and sisters. We gather here today seventy years after the US Supreme Court declared that segregating children by race had no place in public education. It was not so much that nine white men in black robes woke up but it was that millions of Americans white and Black rose up and our nation's conscience cried that it was beneath the promise of the Constitution to inflict the stigma of race, that it was beneath the call of the Scriptures that declares out of one blood God has made all people. And so, responding to that cry the court ruled that school segregation was too low down for the high ideals that we needed to rise to higher ground. We are assembled here today fifty-nine years after Martin Luther King Jr. said the greatest fear of the greedy oligarch in this country was for the masses of black people and white people to form a voting bloc that could fundamentally shift the economic architecture—of this year—of this country.[3]

2. In April 2023, following a mass shooting that killed six people just days prior at the Covenant School in Nashville, Tennessee, members of the Tennessee State House of Representatives Justin Jones, Justin Pearson, and Gloria Johnson protested gun violence and called for gun control legislation in the state capitol chambers and in solidarity with the crowds who had gathered to protest just outside on the Capitol steps. In response, the majority of their colleagues voted to expel Jones and Pearson from the House, while votes for Johnson's expulsion failed. Although neither Jones or Pearson are ordained clergy, they both have clear connections to the Christian tradition, and Jones was, for a time, enrolled as a student at Vanderbilt Divinity School. In response to his expulsion from the statehouse, Jones had the opportunity to defend himself and face questioning from his House colleagues. During the proceedings, Rep. Ryan Williams asks Jones, "One of the questions

---

3. "The Mass Poor People's & Low-Wage Workers' Assembly."

that keeps coming back to my mind that I hope maybe you can answer is: when you say, 'No action, no peace,' what do you mean? What does Representative Jones mean by 'No peace.' Thank you." Jones responds,

> Um, I would invite my colleague from Putnam County to join any protests where that is a very familiar chant; that it usually goes, "No justice, no peace." And I believe the roots of it are—lie in something that Martin Luther King stated that "true peace is not merely the absence of tension, but it is the presence of justice." That's what I was saying . . . is that until we act, there will be no peace in our communities. In addition, I would like to read some context about that chant that comes from Jeremiah 6:14. I'll read the New Living Translation. It says, "They offer superficial treatments for my people's mortal wound. They give assurances of peace where there is no peace." I'll go to the New International Version: "They dress the wound of my people as though it was not serious. Peace, peace, peace, they say where there is no peace." That's what the chant means—is that we have no peace and that until we act, there will be no peace for the thousands of children who came here demanding that we act, who are afraid that if they're in school, they'll be gunned down because you have passed laws to make it easier to get a gun than it is to get health care in this state. You pass laws to make it easier to get a gun than it is to vote in this state and so that there will be no peace in Tennessee until we act on this proliferation of weapons of war in our community. That is the peace I was talking about. That is what I was saying, Representative Williams. Thank you for your question.[4]

These two speakers and the scenarios in which they speak share some similarities. Both speak with precision and power. Both deploy religious language, though in different ways. Both advocate for just action. Yet there are significant fundamental differences to which we should pay deep attention. The goals of their speaking are different. The listeners are different. The ways that they represent faith communities differ. The power granted to the speakers is different. Not every situation in which we speak in the public square will have the same conditions, but these conditions shape the speaking situation. If we fail to attend to the conditions that shape the context of our speaking, then we risk

---

4. "'A Public Lynching': Justin Jones, Black Tennessee Lawmaker, Responds to Expulsion from State House," Democracy Now!, April 7, 2023, YouTube, https://www.youtube.com/watch?v=XvOoLYI3NOc.

failure in our communication. In particular, the conditions of what I call the "communicative situation" depend in part on relationships with listeners and the distribution of power between speaker and listeners.

With respect to preaching, preachers need to understand their place, the preaching context and the relationships they hold, and the power they negotiate in the preaching moment. Understanding these aspects of ourselves leads preachers to a preaching strategy that makes sense for gaining a hearing in the preaching moment. Preachers take different approaches to the biblical text, the design of the sermon, the sermon's content, and the sermon's tone depending on these factors, which are generally predictable in a long-term relationship with a congregation. Thomas Long's comment from the opening pages of *The Witness of Preaching* makes a theological and ecclesiological statement:

> Regardless of where the worship leaders emerge physically and architecturally, theologically it is crucial to remember that we come from within the community of faith and not to it from the outside. Whether we use this door or that one, process down the center aisle or modestly glide to our chairs, it is not nearly as important as remembering that, even though we will now be the leaders of worship, we have come to this task from the midst of the community of faith and not from the outside.[5]

This is easy enough to understand as a *theological* and *ecclesiological* commitment in the context of common worship. However, we know in reality that pastors often feel like outsiders *culturally*, which can be especially apparent in the pulpit. As Nora Tisdale observes of her own time serving four different congregations simultaneously, "Pastoring four churches was much like having four children—each with its own distinctive personality, character, and idiosyncrasies. Consequently, it was not uncommon for the same sermon—preached in four different settings—to elicit four totally different responses from the congregations."[6] In response, Tisdale encourages preachers to adopt an ethnographic lens in order to more fittingly preach to the distinct cultures of congregations.[7]

Things change in the public square. The speaker is likely among a

---

5. Thomas G. Long, *The Witness of Preaching*, 3rd ed. (Westminster John Knox, 2016), 2.
6. Leonora Tubbs Tisdale, *Preaching as Local Theology and Folk Art* (Fortress, 1997), 4.
7. Eunjoo Kim further complexifies understandings of culture in her work. See Eunjoo Mary Kim, *Preaching in an Age of Globalization* (Westminster John Knox, 2010); Kim, *Christian Preaching and Worship in Multicultural Contexts: A Practical Theological Approach* (Pueblo Books, 2017).

greater diversity of cultural representation than in a typical congregation. This is generally not a large hurdle, since the communicative situation engenders a common interest. But the speaker is not always the insider theologically and ecclesiologically, though one might be among those who share the same faith values and general sense of the ordering of ministry. When thinking about questions of social, political, and economic forces, in connection with the status of religious groups and religious leaders, we are also led to think about how *power* enters the equation and, more specifically, our power as speakers in relationship to those who have gathered and in relationship to other stakeholders. So how do we understand our place and plan appropriately? Because understanding one's place and responding appropriately can make all the difference in helping identify a fitting and effective speaking strategy, this chapter seeks to explore the question *What is my place in the communicative situation?*

CONTEXT AND RELATIONSHIPS IN PUBLIC PROCLAMATION

To What Extent Do I Represent My Faith Community?

When I talk about public proclamation in my class, I often use a video showing the 2017 press conference launch of the Poor People's Campaign. There, crowded around a podium, are somewhere around twenty-five to thirty people, including cochairs Liz Theoharis and William J. Barber II, along with leaders from approximately a dozen Christian and Jewish denominations, public policy and faith-based advocacy groups, and unions.[8] These representatives stand side by side (literally and figuratively), many dressed in clergy collars or stoles, as they are introduced to give roughly two-minute speeches that pledge their support for the work of the campaign. The speeches are energizing, which, given the occasion, is exactly the right tone. Each speaker names their role, their perspective, and why their particular denomination or group will be invested in the work of the Poor People's Campaign. Some draw from the Hebrew Bible or Christian Scriptures as justification and common language. In a classroom with many denominations represented among

---

8. "Poor, Disenfranchised, Clergy and Allies Launch Movement for Moral Revival in America," Repairers of the Breach, December 4, 2017, YouTube, https://www.youtube.com/watch?v=eyRdJjXO4wk.

my students, I want them to see their faith tradition represented and to see the power of an ecumenical and interfaith movement (a "moral movement," as Barber says).

As students watch, they are drawn to the embodied dynamics of the speeches, or to the metaphors developed, or to the use of faith-rooted language. On one occasion, a student posed a particularly insightful question that moved in a different direction. With consternation in their voice, and speaking about the faith leaders, the student essentially said, "That's all well and good. But these people are moderators, general ministers, general secretaries, and bishops of their denominations. They represent denominations and are paid to do so. But what about me in a local congregation? To what extent do I represent my own views and to what extent do I represent my congregation when I am engaging in public proclamation, especially when it comes to issues of social justice?" This is a fantastic question, one that many clergy might ask.

If pastors account for the culture of a congregation, as Tisdale and Kim advise us to do, then we will recognize that the great majority of our congregations contain a multitude of views on social justice issues and theological and doctrinal commitments. As theologically and ecclesiologically idyllic as Long's view of the minister emerging from the congregation is, the work of negotiating that place and identity in practice is something quite different. Thus, to speak in public on issues of social importance as a representative of a particular congregation can complicate relationships with those who might have contrary views. This is true especially for those who have systems in which ministers' calls are congregational, as opposed to a placement-based system—though, to be clear, a placement system does not eliminate the possibility for difficult dynamics.

Framing Ministry and Relationships for Public Proclamation

My response, I am sorry to say, does not offer a universal answer. I do have three recommendations that can help negotiate an understanding of the place where clergy stand when it comes to public proclamation. I encourage pastors who do the work of public proclamation to (1) know their theologies of ministry, (2) form deep relationships among the church community that can weather disagreement, and (3) find and nurture supportive relationships within the congregation (especially in leadership roles) and beyond it.

First, when I urge pastors to know their theologies of ministry, I am particularly interested in those aspects that justify their participation in public life *in clergy roles*. For instance, in the "Theological Foundations and Policies and Criteria for the Ordering of Ministry of the Christian Church (Disciples of Christ)," which is my tradition, a few key ideas are helpful. In the section titled "The Character of Ordained Ministry," item 2 outlines an aspect of ordained ministry that it calls "representative ministry." By this, the document means "those who accept the ministry of the Word, sacrament, and mission are responsible for re-presenting (showing forth) to the world and to all baptized Christians the character of Christ's ministry and witness. A central task of such representative ministry is personally and publicly to point the church to its dependence on Jesus Christ, who is the source of its faith, mission, and unity."[9] Here the document points to a *public* role for ministers. This role might be interpreted either narrowly or broadly in community and might not be clear in terms of social justice, whereas in other situations there would be ample support for bearing witness in public. However, the document is clear later in the section "Ministerial Code of Ethics," subsection "Relationships to the Community and the Wider Church." There it states that part of the work of ministers is "participating responsibly in the life and work of my community, bearing prophetic witness to the gospel of Jesus Christ, and working towards a just and morally responsible society."[10] Thus, according to the principles of the Christian Church (Disciples of Christ), the minister's first responsibility is to be a representative ministry of Jesus Christ and not a representative ministry of the congregation. Of course, each denominational tradition articulates these ideas in different ways; differences and divergences will occur. I do not want readers to come away thinking that a hard line of "knowing what the book says" is sufficient for conversations with people who may not be supportive of a pastor's public proclamation. This hardly develops healthy congregational understanding of the minister's role or a minister's relationship to the congregation.

Before moving on, a word about free church traditions. In some free church traditions, official theological foundations and policies might not exist at all. In these congregations, expectations are bound by local

---

9. "Theological Foundations and Policies and Criteria for the Ordering of Ministry of the Christian Church (Disciples of Christ)," 2014, lines 434–39, https://cdn.disciples.org/wp-content/uploads/2014/07/06162557/TFPCOM-Final.pdf.

10. "Theological Foundations and Policies," lines 1739–41.

tradition or with church leaders. Some of my students are perplexed by the ways their traditions articulate the separation of church and state and the implications for clergy in the work of public proclamation. If this is the case, I would invite you to think through your own understandings (often with support from the biblical witness) and then move into the next recommendations with substantive conversation.

Whether there is agreement, disagreement, or a mix of both in a congregation, forming deep relationships that can weather disagreement is crucial. While this might sound obvious, I want to suggest that this recommendation comes from a commitment shared by many that the church is and should be a "community of conversation."[11] Ronald Allen suggests that "a conversational church respects the Bible and tradition, and listens carefully to their voices, adopting those perspectives that are life-giving while having the freedom to critique and even turn away from aspects of the Bible and tradition that work against God's purposes. The conversation includes Scripture and tradition while going beyond those voices."[12]

Focusing specifically on the minister, John McClure outlines the dangers of entrenchment and divisive oppositional frameworks, particularly as they manifest in models of ministry focused on what he calls "narrative entrenchment." These feed from and into our already polarized culture. Instead, he advocates for ministers "who are able to relate and connect worldviews and negotiate shared meaning and truth *across* differences on behalf of the common flourishing of all." McClure summarizes his proposal this way: "Ministry, therefore, is a process of becoming ever-better conversation partners in service to the gospel. It is this image of minister as conversation partner that is needed in our current situation in which our obsession with living into wholly consistent narratives or worldviews is driving wedges between people in the church and in the larger society."[13] This compelling insight may seem opposed to the kind of public proclamation we might imagine (here I harken back to popular imaginings of "the prophetic"), in which a lone speaker—the minister—speaks in decisive ways about whatever has prompted the communicative situation. We would do well to imagine public proclamation as part of a matrix of *ongoing* conversations in the

---

11. O. Wesley Allen, John McClure, and Ronald J. Allen, eds., *Under the Oak Tree: The Church as Community of Conversation in a Conflicted and Pluralistic World* (Cascade Books, 2013).
12. Ronald J. Allen, "The Church as Community of Conversation," in *Under the Oak Tree*, 10.
13. John S. McClure, "The Minister as Conversation Partner," in *Under the Oak Tree*, 28–29.

congregation and community, rather than a one-off or instance of speaking that is final and unrelated to other conversations, both with respect to interpersonal relationships and in the conversation that we characterize as preaching and common worship.[14] Reframing public proclamation as part of the minister's and church's ongoing conversation emphasizes relationality and a revised sense of authority.[15] Even when we know that there might be disagreement, this approach to ministry predisposes us to the work of cultivating relationships in and beyond the congregation that prioritize "a shared human quest for truth and values . . . [and] for the meaning of the gospel in today's world."[16]

The third recommendation is to find and nurture supportive relationships within and beyond the congregation. In the previous chapter, I referenced the Lone Ranger prophet model. As Jacobsen points out, not only does this model lack biblical nuance, but I would suggest it also serves as a recipe for burnout, loneliness, and conflict in community. Anyone who enters the work of public proclamation knows that only rarely is it about the moment of speaking. The moment of speaking flows from, and is connected to, organizing and resourcing. That critical work can nurture and support public proclamation as stories are shared, hopes emerge, new ideas come to life, and victories and disappointments are allowed to surface.

In addition, finding supportive members of the congregation who will offer support, advice, and correction when needed is likewise necessary for the work of public proclamation, especially with respect to congregational leadership. While carefully avoiding the formation of cliques or groups that wrongfully exert pressure on or divide the congregation, ministers should cultivate relationships with those in congregational leadership who remind others in the congregation that public proclamation is the work of ministry, that it is connected to the witness of the local and wider manifestations of the church, and that it stems from the theological foundations identified earlier. In addition, finding supportive relationships beyond the congregation can help with feelings of isolation, disappointment, fear, and so on.

---

14. See especially O. Wesley Allen Jr., *The Homiletic of All Believers: A Conversational Approach to Proclamation and Preaching* (Westminster John Knox, 2005); Ronald J. Allen and O. Wesley Allen Jr., *The Sermon without End: A Conversational Approach to Preaching* (Abingdon, 2015).

15. See Richard William Voelz, *Preaching to Teach: Inspire People to Think and Act* (Abingdon, 2019), 51–67.

16. McClure, "The Minister as Conversation Partner," 32.

POWER AND PLACE

What I have said so far about the public self has described nothing regarding the actual strategy of public proclamation. Our discussion here, in addition to our grounding in the previous chapter, has served to form the solid footing of understanding who we are and the places from which we speak. In this section, I want to continue to build on this understanding, but with an eye toward how our sense of power in place might lead us to choose different strategies for public proclamation.

In order to do so, a helpful conversation partner is theologian Miriam Perkins, who observes shifts in Martin Luther King Jr.'s speeches throughout his public ministry. King's relationships to power and change agents, as well as his relationship to oppositional forces, changed as society changed, as new dimensions to his own understanding of justice changed, and as his contexts for speaking changed. Understanding "prophetic voice to be the capacity to speak with moral and theological vision in pursuit of social justice from non-dominant standpoints," Perkins notes that "across his lifetime, King exercised an increasingly more forceful [prophetic] voice."[17] This important clarification leads us away from thinking of King's speeches as somewhat uniform and consistent in terms of communicational strategy. While King might have been drawing from the same well of rhetorical ornamentation and style across the years and in different situations, the communicational strategy vis-à-vis his listeners necessarily adapted. According to Perkins, we do well to see King's speaking as "dynamic" and "situational." We should also note that King negotiated space as an African American cisgender, heterosexual man who was university educated and middle class; thus, his social location added a great deal to the possibilities for public speech, whereas others from even more minoritized social locations might be rendered "mute" by "civic and social forces."[18] Perkins analyzes King's speeches with an eye toward the relationship between two key elements: power and communicational strategy. In doing so, she helps us recognize that King's sense of situational power affected his communicational strategy. As a result, when we understand that these work in tandem, we, too, can choose effective strategies for our own instances of public proclamation, as well as for "communities of overlapping voices and practices."[19]

---

17. Miriam Y. (Miriam Yvonne) Perkins, "The Praxis of Prophetic Voice: Martin Luther King, Jr. and Strategies for Resistance," *Black Theology* 17, no. 3 (2019): 242, https://doi.org/10.1080/14769948.2019.1688089.
18. Perkins, 243.
19. Perkins, 243.

Three Types of Power, Three Communicational Strategies

Prior to unpacking the ways that power and communicational strategy can work together effectively, we should gain a basic understanding of the three types of power Perkins describes. In terms of power, Perkins offers three positions of the speaker's relationship to power. First is "proximal," for "those situations in which we raise a viewpoint that challenges the status quo as a person who is 'in the room' and able to speak as an acknowledged participant and collaborator." As a brief example, we can look to the example of William J. Barber II and the Poor People's Campaign related at the outset of the chapter. Barber and others were gathered together in a group of like-minded people who shared experiences or commitments in challenging the status quo of the political system. Perkins calls the second position of power "intermediate," which is characterized by "when a person is 'in the room' as a voice for change but not a decision maker; power for change rests with a reluctant interlocutor." Another quick example might be the city council or school board meeting, in which we might be present as a valued member of the community, but our presence does not guarantee a decision in favor for whatever we might be advocating. Third is what Perkins calls "peripheral power." As we might imagine, the distance from decision-making and a favorable hearing increases. This kind of power "designates those situations where respectful dialogue is not an effective avenue for change because of oppression or suppression of non-dominant standpoints."[20] For a quick example here, we might think of a group of clergy and allies on the steps of city hall or the state capitol before or after a protest or rally and in which there is known opposition and no seat at the table.

Proximal Power and Standpoint

Drawing from various fields of study, Perkins highlights three types of situational communication strategies that function as appropriate matches for the types of power just named. First among these is "standpoint," which pairs with proximal power. According to Perkins, "Standpoint theory proposes that cultural and social context, particularly the social groups to which persons belong, shapes what human beings know and understand about the world. One's place in society, and especially locations of belonging, foregrounds certain perspectives." In terms of communicational

20. Perkins, 243.

approach, the speaker highlights their standpoint (their experiences and social location) "as a reflection of shared social distance from power in a culture."[21] Remembering that the speaker identifies as someone "in the room," they should name their standpoint as something that is shared with others as they move toward their communicational goals.

As noted earlier, Perkins connects these combinations to moments in King's public proclamation. To demonstrate what she means by proximal power and standpoint, she points to King's work during the Montgomery bus boycott. More specifically referring to his speech accepting leadership of the Montgomery Improvement Association, "King drew upon these resisting strategies of standpoint to situate the decision for a bus boycott within the history of the African American struggle for dignity . . . outlin[ing] the experience of African Americans as patrons of the bus system, who pay the same fare as Whites, while Whites are never asked to surrender a seat. In the homiletic spirit of the slave preacher, King tied the boycott to abolition, exile, and liberation." King speaks as the "outsider-within," who uses his distinct social location within an oppressed and minoritized group to create an ethos and group identity that pushes toward justice with the collective goals of organizing.[22]

Perkins's categorization of this approach is extremely helpful, as is the concrete example with King. At the same time, we should not limit our thinking to racialized communicative situations. Indeed, as a feminist, Perkins picks up on this and notes that "communication is shaped by a nexus of identity markers. These include primary and secondary markers unique to each communicator and are juxtaposed with attributes that overlap with multiple markers of belonging. They include such factors as age, race, religion, nationality, language, sexual orientation, economic status, education, physical ability, and gender."[23] Though Perkins does not use the term, more commonly now we would use "intersectionality"[24] to describe what Perkins names, meaning the ways that marginalized identities overlap.

In my opening vignette depicting the Poor People's Campaign rally for voting, this is exactly what the gathering as a whole, and the speeches in particular, were aiming to achieve. That is to say, the public proclamation sought to galvanize low-wage and impoverished voters across racialized,

---

21. Perkins, 244–45.
22. Perkins, 245.
23. Perkins, 246. Standpoint theory has been common in feminist discourses for some time.
24. Kimberle Crenshaw, "Mapping the Margins: Intersectionality, Identity Politics, and Violence against Women of Color," *Stanford Law Review* 43, no. 6 (1991), https://doi.org/10.2307/1229039.

gender, and identity markers, as well as people of various (and no) faiths who see themselves as "moral voices" who are challenged by a powerful force that often uses religious language to dominate others through political and economic means. Barber seeks to unify a coalition of people across minoritized social locations and would-be allies, speaking out of his own standpoint but also of those that are shared beyond a racialized perspective, particularly along the lines of class. His primary audience is not those in power but those who are gathered. When Barber uses the language of "higher ground," "rise up," "swing vote," "stigma," "segregation," or "greedy oligarch," he is appealing to minoritized and marginalized standpoints that can cross lines to form a collective ethos of resistance and organizing. In addition, Barber continues to connect the work of the contemporary iteration of the Poor People's Campaign to the historical legacy of the civil rights movement.

Two additional notes on proximal power and standpoint are important to raise. First, those of us from more privileged social locations might wonder if our privilege excludes us from this strategy for public proclamation. If proximal power means that the speaker is located in the room, sharing experiences of marginalization with those who are gathered, then how do we proceed? To this, Perkins offers at least a partial answer. She suggests that "for would-be White allies of racial justice, standpoint calls for inviting non-White people into proximal spaces where their own standpoints can be both heard and amplified."[25] In other words, Perkins suggests that those who move through the world in privileged positions should know when to "pass the mic" so that marginalized perspectives gain the hearing they deserve. But there is another dimension that lies somewhat dormant in Perkins's article. She points to King's own points of privilege in terms of social status, education, and occupation, and, perhaps most importantly in this case, his class. King "had not ridden the bus in Montgomery. He had a car, and he was putting the car in the service of the boycott and asking others with cars to do the same."[26] Though King was not entirely able to identify with the marginalization that many shared along the lines of class, he pointed to what he did share with them. This kind of strategy, especially with the kind of intersectional analysis of social location and identity we have today, can be an effective tool. In essence, a speaker might carefully and sensitively acknowledge in

---

25. Perkins, "Praxis of Prophetic Voice," 247.
26. Perkins, 246.

some way, "I do not know what it is like to experience *X*, but I do know what it is like to experience *Y*." To underscore: this takes care so as not to minimize the marginalization of others, nor to collapse experiences into each other. As Perkins notes, "This recognition can support activism when communicators recognize their nexus of power markers, stressing some and downplaying others, to gain credibility and challenge the standpoints of opponents."[27] It can be especially helpful to name that we speak from a place of privilege and seek solidarity when we do not share the marginalized experiences but have the opportunity to speak.

Second, I do not believe that we necessarily need to limit our use of standpoint theory to traditional identity markers and understanding of social location, nor the communicative situation to oppositional moments that encourage resistance. Perkins is focused on social justice movements through the lens of King, which is extremely helpful. We might also think of how natural disasters or communal crises generate shared experiences that might lead ministers to places of proximal power and a standpoint strategy. I often give students role-playing scenarios in which they are asked to play the part of clergy and community leaders who have experienced a hurricane or tornado in their community. I set up mock interviews with a former local news reporter. When students speak as a group, without fail they emphasize the collective identity of those who have suffered disaster and use that as a springboard for calling the viewers or listeners to participate in efforts to support the community as they are able, both in the moment of crisis and in a more sustained fashion. This understanding of proximal power and standpoint is appropriate as well.

Intermediate Power and Strategic Interaction

Perkins's second combination operates on the sense of intermediate power of the speaker, who is in the room yet does not have power as a decision maker and faces a reluctant change agent. Paired with this type of power is what sociologist Erving Goffman calls "'strategic interaction' in which a person presents and protects an image of self. . . . Strategic interaction takes place when 'two or more parties . . . find themselves in a well-structured situation of mutual impingement where each party must

---

27. Perkins, 246.

make a move and where every possible move carries fateful implications for all of the parties.'"[28] To this, Stella Ting-Toomey and Atsuko Kurogi add what they call "facework," which are communicative strategies used to "regulate their social dignity and to support or challenge the other's social dignity."[29] Summarizing facework, Perkins says of King's interactions with President Lyndon Johnson in and around 1965, as well as the attempts to march over the Edmund Pettus Bridge, as "discerning how hard to push one's opponent without causing him or her to lose face."[30] With respect to King, this required various strategies of how to interact with and characterize the constellation of players such as Johnson, George Wallace, and other elected officials across state and local government in Alabama, law enforcement, and racist citizens. I do not detail here the ways that Perkins describes how King used public communication strategies with these officials in pursuit of a voting rights law and the Pettus Bridge march. Suffice it to say, this communicational strategy demands a delicate balance of portraying an opponent or those in power with a gentle enough image—or appealing to their better nature—and applying critique without losing the opportunity for dialogue and the possibility of change. The idea, of course, is to generate pressure on an opponent for the purpose of change while not antagonizing or demonizing them in the process, and "simultaneously disarming their strategies to shut down active protest."[31]

This kind of strategic interaction and facework means that those who speak must have a significant premeditated and coordinated strategy of what it means to negotiate this place of intermediate power, as well as a "feel for the game" and ways to characterize and nudge decision makers in ways that leave open the path for change. Speakers should be aware of larger strategies that connect to organizing goals beyond the speaking moment. A misstep could shut down the possibility of relationships that could lead to change. The LGBTQIA+ advocacy group I worked with was in response to the Christian liberal arts college from which I graduated. Years after I graduated, the school's administration engaged in significant anti-LGBTQIA+ behavior. Many of us who graduated from the school

---

28. Erving Goffman, *Strategic Interaction* (University of Pennsylvania Press, 1969), 100–101, quoted in Perkins, 247–48.
29. Stella Ting-Toomey and Atsuko Kurogi, "Facework Competence in Intercultural Conflict: An Updated Face-Negotiation Theory," *International Journal of Intercultural Relations* 22, no. 2 (1988): 188.
30. Perkins, "The Praxis of Prophetic Voice," 248.
31. Perkins, 249.

(intermediate power) felt that these actions betrayed an institutional ethos that had taught us values of love and acceptance, the inherent worth and dignity for all human beings, and the power of community even in disagreement. Part of our public appeal for the administration to engage with our group and to do the work of repair was communicated in the press and, eventually, in face-to-face conversation with the administration. We sought to communicate two ideas: (1) we were operating out of love for the school that had so deeply shaped us, and (2) we simply wanted the school to live into the values that we were taught during our time there—values that had made our lives rich and meaningful. This appeal to values and our love for the school were attempts to engage in facework with the school's leadership. Though our strategy shifted over time due to their recalcitrance, I would describe this strategy as intermediate power and strategic interaction through facework.

Peripheral Power and Co-cultural Resistance

Perkins's final combination is that of peripheral power—those situations in which nondominant voices have been shut down by those in power—and "co-cultural resistance." This term emerges from sociological research that analyzes "communication strategies that dominant cultures use to mute non-dominant voices, and strategies that counteract this muting."[32] Here, co-cultural theory seeks to understand how those who have power and dominance control the terms of engagement, so to speak, for how communication happens and what can be communicated. In essence, the powerful "govern social interaction. It follows that those in the dominant social group have a 'muting' effect on co-cultural voices; these voices cannot necessarily be silenced, but they can be made to appear non-existent."[33] As a result, those who are in the nondominant group (or co-cultural voices) must become increasingly innovative in their communication.

As an example of this type of communication, Perkins points to King's speech[34] titled "Beyond Vietnam: A Time to Break Silence," delivered April 4, 1967, at Riverside Church in New York City for the multifaith Clergy

32. Perkins, 251.
33. Perkins, 251.
34. Some call this a speech while others call it a sermon. Since the occasion was for a multifaith conference outside the context of Christian worship, despite its physical location at Riverside Church, I designate it as a speech or instance of public proclamation. Because of their seating capacity and the

and Laymen Concerned about Vietnam conference. King's opposition to the Vietnam War was something that progressed over his public ministry. His observation of the ways that young impoverished Black men sent to fight in Vietnam intersected with the work for civil rights that pushed King to the margins of civil rights movement leaders and the broader American public. In the eyes of many civil rights movement leaders, King had shifted his attention away from the main goal, while for the American public the war was widely supported. Recognizing his place and his stance on Vietnam, King made communicative choices that recognized his peripheral power.

Mark Orbe identifies six factors that influence the communicative choices of those who are in nondominant (co-cultural) groups. In brief, these include the following:

1. *Preferred outcome*: Speakers assess what they want to happen as a result of their speaking. Typically, these options are either assimilation (fitting in), accommodation (advocating that the dominant system accommodate to the co-cultural group), or separation (rejecting the possibilities for common bonds with the dominant group).[35]
2. *Field of experience*: By this, Orbe means that speakers make different decisions based on their life experiences that affect the ways a speaker might communicate with a dominant group.[36]
3. *Abilities*: Here Orbe suggests that speakers have different abilities for interpersonal and public communication that allows them to identify with, mirror (or the more current popular term "code switch"), or generally engage in communicative practices different than their norm.[37]
4. *Situational context*: Speakers must select communicative practices that fit the physical setting and understand both who is in the space and the relational dynamics that are present.[38]
5. *Perceived costs and rewards*: Speakers choose different strategies based on how it will affect them (both as individuals and as

---

rootedness of the movement in ecclesial communities, such speeches commonly took place in church buildings throughout the US South and other regions in the civil rights era.

35. Mark P. Orbe, *Constructing Co-cultural Theory: An Explication of Culture, Power, and Communication* (SAGE, 1997), 89–93.

36. Orbe, 93–95.

37. Orbe, 95–98.

38. Orbe, 98–101.

a collective), according to what they might gain and lose in a particular communicative situation.[39]

6. *Communication approach*: Orbe proposes that speakers in co-cultural groups choose approaches on a spectrum of "nonassertive," "assertive," and "aggressive." Nonassertive practices are those that seem "inhibited and nonconfrontational." Aggressive practices are "*perceived* as hurtfully expressive, self-promoting, and assuming the control over the choices of others." Assertive practices ride the line between these two positions and "encompass self-enhancing, expressive behavior that takes into account both self and others' needs."[40]

Orbe presents a variety of factors for co-cultural communication that might shape an approach of someone with peripheral power. These are helpful markers, and Perkins suggests that King's speech demonstrates "an assertive separation from support for the war suggest[ing] that what cannot be *practically* changed can, nevertheless, be *verbally, visually, and bodily* opposed."[41] In the opening moves of the speech, King says of his opposition: "Some of us who have already begun to break the silence of the night have found that the calling to speak is often a vocation of agony, but we must speak."[42] Just in this one line, we can see that King recognizes the opposition, his separation from the dominant group, and the costs of speaking.

To point to a more contemporary example, Rep. Justin Jones's speech on the statehouse floor shows an example of someone who has been pushed into a nondominant group by virtue of his expulsion. Jones is faced with an antagonist (only one in this example, but there are others) and responds with what I would call an assertive approach that draws on his ability to mirror many forms of Black sacred rhetoric but also on his ability to connect the language of protest and the words of Scripture (abilities, field of experience). Jones has a clear goal of defending himself but also of a sense of separation. In essence, Jones suggests that Rep. Williams's professed Christianity predisposes him to participate in protest and to raise the chant "No justice, no peace" but

---

39. Orbe, 101–4.
40. Orbe, 104–6.
41. Perkins, "The Praxis of Prophetic Voice," 253.
42. Martin Luther King Jr., *A Testament of Hope: The Essential Writings and Speeches*, ed. James M. Washington (repr., HarperOne, 2003), 231.

also acknowledges that there will be no peace until just action is taken on gun violence in the statehouse (separation).

CONCLUSION

Perkins suggests that from her perspective, analyzing King's public proclamation helps answer the question "How do would-be allies develop the desire and courageous capacity to participate in social protest? Cultivating a voice of moral courage and identifying the strategies that embody it include observing, naming, and reflecting upon dynamics of power in communication."[43] Perkins's work highlights the necessity of understanding not only place, as I suggested earlier in this chapter, but also power's effect on the range of communicative choices we might make along the way in our own public proclamation. This kind of analysis and discernment can make us wiser and more dynamic in the communicative choices we make and, as a result, more effective in our public proclamation. With a better understanding of ourselves, our role(s) and power, and our place as those who engage in public proclamation, we turn now to think about how we understand the contexts and goals of public proclamation.

EXERCISE YOUR VOICE

—Take a look at your denominational tradition's expressions of clergy roles. What do they suggest about the work of public proclamation? If you are congregational clergy, how do you experience your sense of place in the public square, and how have you negotiated or hope to negotiate that identity in your congregation?

—If you are more experienced in public proclamation, choose an instance of your speaking and identify some of the contextual and power dynamics, as well as features of your communicative approach using the categories outlined in this chapter. In retrospect, what went well and made your speaking effective, based on your understanding of the dynamics and communicative approaches discussed here? Do you recognize anything that would have made your speaking more effective had you known it and taken it into account?

---

43. Perkins, "The Praxis of Prophetic Voice," 253.

—If you are less experienced in public proclamation, imagine a scenario in your community in which you could or would be a likely speaker. List some of the contextual and power dynamics that would affect you in that communicative situation. What kinds of communicative approaches and understanding of power would help you in this scenario?

3
Understanding the Contexts and Strategic Goals of Public Proclamation

In the previous chapter, I emphasized the importance of making sense of ourselves for the work of public proclamation. As we build toward practices that can sustain public proclamation, this kind of self-examination and discernment about ourselves forms an indispensable step. As we move the circle of the speaking context wider than just ourselves as speakers, the previous chapter and this chapter work in tandem, because communication does not take place in a vacuum. When we make our way into the public sphere, we must account for the ways that the context of our speaking affects not only us—just as we did when we looked at the role of power—but also the communicative situation as a whole. In speaking about community organizing, Loretta Pyles acknowledges that "it is impossible to engage in strategic processes, analyze sources of power, and implement tactics without having an understanding of the context and community and the key issues identified by impacted communities."[1] That is to say, before we act—and in our case, speak—we need to understand context. As we seek a better contextual understanding, we are working toward being able to speak in ways that are more likely to gain a hearing among our would-be allies and those who may oppose us. This chapter focuses on two questions that continue with the preparatory work for public proclamation. The first of these is, *How do I understand what's going on here?*

---

1. Loretta Pyles, *Progressive Community Organizing: Transformative Practice in a Globalizing World* (Taylor and Francis, 2021), 221.

The second question moves toward the beginning stages of shaping the message, whether that message will be fully scripted or not. Once we have laid the foundational pieces regarding ourselves and our contexts, we want to be able to clearly articulate what we hope will happen as a result of our speaking. Those results should be wholly consistent with the larger strategic goals of the movement, organization, local community, or congregation for which we speak. In order to achieve our goals and avoid disruption or harm, public proclamation should always be integrated with an overall communicative and organization strategy. This integrative approach means that while public proclamation may serve significant purposes as a strategic part of organizing work, it is not that work's singular focus. Thus, the second question we need to answer is, *What is the strategic goal of our communicative situation?* To answer these questions of context and goal/purpose, we adapt and supplement some (perhaps) familiar homiletical tools.

At the outset, I should say that this kind of work on the front end may seem time consuming and labor intensive, and like it poses barriers to responding to certain situations with immediacy or doing so more extemporaneously. I do not want to prevent anyone from responding as quickly as possible. My goal is not to burden the process. Emergency situations might preclude the kind of preparation I describe in the previous chapter and in this one. At the same time, I also want to suggest that this kind of preparation can help foster a more comprehensive understanding of whatever situation might prompt public proclamation, deepening our ability to effect change. Additionally, this kind of preparation can help us to move more fluidly and quickly when called on to speak and to speak in ways that account both for those who are listening and for the connections we should make to larger strategic purposes. Finally, I suggest that while we want to be intentional with this kind of preparation, it can also become less cumbersome and more intuitive through repeated use (or alternatively, can provide a good back-to-basics approach when needed).

UNDERSTANDING THE PUBLIC CONTEXT

As I noted in the previous chapter, when Nora Tisdale experienced preaching to four different congregations, it raised the stakes for attending to contextual, cultural realities of sermon listeners in congregations. According to Tisdale,

A focus upon "the cultural" in preaching pushes the pastor toward the kind of priestly listening that moves beyond the bounds of universals and individuals to consider communal traits and characteristics that unite members with one another and with other societal and ecclesial communities of belief and practice. . . . A focus upon the cultural in preaching encourages the preacher to address the congregation *as* congregation—a distinctive and unique community of faith that is, itself, in certain respects, "like no others."[2]

In many respects, this is what we are after in the preparatory work of public proclamation.

Some communities that form the context for public proclamation are similar to congregations. That is, they will meet regularly and have significant structures that form and support a subcultural identity. In this respect, I think of a multifaith community organizing group in the city where I live called RISC (Richmonders Involved to Strengthen our Communities), which is part of the DART network of congregation-based community organizations.[3] Throughout the chapter, I refer to the work of RISC and its public proclamation. However, some communicative situations are often more temporary, ad hoc, and more permeable than congregations, whether they have significant organizations that support them or not. Here, I would refer to the Poor People's Campaign rallies I have drawn on elsewhere or, more loosely, emergency moments of public proclamation born out of protest where significant organizing work may precede whatever event has precipitated the communicative situation. Or conversely, the communicative situation might serve as a beginning point for organizing. Either way, when people gather, they in some ways form, as the quote from Tisdale says, "a distinctive and unique community . . . that is, itself, in certain respects, 'like no others.'" When we plan our speaking in these communities, it is helpful to have some understanding of what makes those who gather that distinctive and unique community. Some readers are familiar with the term "congregational exegesis," which covers analytical tools that help us gain a better understanding of the congregation as a system. This section of the chapter transfers some of these tools for the work of public proclamation as a way of engaging in contextual and social analysis that sets the stage for public proclamation. Some readers are more familiar with tools that come from community organizing circles. Other readers have had no exposure to those kinds of tools.

2. Leonora Tubbs Tisdale, *Preaching as Local Theology and Folk Art* (Fortress, 1997), 12.
3. RISC, "RISC," accessed July 15, 2024, https://www.riscrichmond.org/.

My use of congregational exegesis tools over those that might originate in community organizing is, first, simply for the purpose of providing easily relatable or transferrable devices for those who have had primary experiences leading or working with congregations. Second, the terms are useful because many readers understand congregational contexts as part of the systems that they are addressing in public proclamation. I draw on the work of community organizing later in this chapter.

Wide View of Context

In their book *Studying Congregations*, Nancy Ammerman, Jackson Carroll, Carl Dudley, and William McKinney propose four "frames" or perspectives for studying congregations. These frames use different approaches to analyze the information gathered about congregations to "facilitate understanding" of a congregation and its situation.[4] I suggest that using these four frames can provide what I here call a "wide view of context."[5] By this, I mean that the frames can help us understand how an instance of public proclamation might both be affected by and affect a larger cultural context. With this understanding, we can gain a more detailed understanding of what is going on and how our public proclamation can play a role in helping us achieve our strategic goals (more on this later). While we are not studying congregations, of course, these familiar tools can help us develop a picture of how public proclamation participates in a social system, with the actors and influences that are part of it.

The Ecological Frame

In describing the ecological frame, the authors suggest that "to use an ecological frame is to see the congregation as an organism in an environment in which there are many other organisms that together make up the social and religious world."[6] In other words, congregations do not stand alone as impermeable organizations but interact with a variety of

---

4. Nancy Ammerman et al., eds., *Studying Congregations: A New Handbook* (Abingdon, 1998), 14.
5. Sally Brown and Luke Powery also use this terminology but in somewhat different ways. See Sally A. Brown and Luke A. Powery, *Ways of the Word: Learning to Preach for Your Time and Place* (Fortress, 2016), 114–17.
6. Ammerman et al., *Studying Congregations*, 14.

social, religious, political, and economic forces. Congregations are both influenced by and influence these forces, which are operative at the local, national, and global levels. As the authors note, "although your context does not determine your congregation's commitments, it does provide the setting within which you must make decisions."[7] This serves as an important connection to public proclamation.

When considering the ecological frame for public proclamation, speakers will certainly be aware of the issue(s) that prompt the communicative event. However, if the issue(s) is seen in isolation—or worse, spoken about in isolation—we do a disservice to listeners. We are better off to see how a presenting issue exists in connection to the wider ecology. For instance, if we are summoned to speak in the aftermath of a hurricane, then we would do well to step back and recognize that hurricanes and the response to them exist in an ecology that is affected by social, religious, political, and economic forces (power). Social, in that communities are bound and fragmented in certain ways, and response may differ according to different needs, abilities, and privileges that exist in that community. Religious, in that different theological understandings of why hurricanes occur exist within communities, and faith communities respond to natural disasters in varied ways, whether that be more insular or communal, more or less charity-driven, or from the approach of communal restoration. With regard to political forces, communities have different response efforts based on their understanding of climate change (both in repair and prevention), and community responses and resources often differ in regard to race and class. Finally, economic forces undoubtedly play a role in disaster response and often in connection to political forces. Who can rebuild? How quickly are resources released and to whom? Who has the means to rebuild quickly? These questions and more suggest that economic forces play a role in what it means to respond to a hurricane. The following are a list of important, but certainly not exhaustive, questions to answer:

—What social, religious, political, or economic forces have caused the situation to emerge?
—Who, if anyone, has benefited from this situation or stands to benefit, and why?
—Who is suffering or impacted and why/how?
—What are the social, religious, political, or economic obstacles toward solidarity, healing, and justice?

---

7. Ammerman et al., 14.

—What are the social, religious, political, or economic forces that might lead toward solidarity, healing, and justice?

Now, will a speaker be able to address all these aspects in a communicative event? Of course not. No instance of public proclamation can be comprehensive with regard to the ecological frame. But this does not nullify our need for a more comprehensive analysis. Recognizing that instances of public proclamation occur within the ecological frame helps speakers focus their communication in specific directions to speak effectively to listeners and achieve strategic goals and more specific communicative purposes (the latter I address in the next chapter). Seeing public proclamation with a lay of the land helps us recognize places to focus in our speaking, gaps and biases in our speaking (and among those listening), and points of connection that have yet to be made or need emphasizing.

The Culture Frame

The culture frame "asks you to imagine the congregation you are studying as a group that has invented ways of being together that are uniquely its own. Even if much of what the congregation's members do has been borrowed from the larger culture, their very being together over time has given them a distinct identity."[8] The authors of *Studying Congregations* suggest a number of factors that constitute a congregation's culture: rituals, training, work, play, artifacts, the stories it tells about itself, symbols and myths, and the peculiarities of the language it uses together. Long-term members of congregations often see the elements of the cultural frame either as natural (if they see them at all), while newcomers recognize the cultural frame through what makes a congregation distinctive or similar to communities of faith to which they previously belonged ("The pastor in my old church used the same benediction as you do!").

When thinking about the cultural frame with regard to public proclamation, we might encounter some difficulty. The situations that prompt public proclamation are not the same as those that prompt preaching (or other types of communication) in congregations. Accordingly, the communities that gather for public proclamation can be wildly varied. On the one hand, some might occur in an emergency situation and may never gather again. Public proclamation might not be an ongoing

---

8. Ammerman et al., 15.

need. Or perhaps the instance of public proclamation comes through a TV interview or publicized press conference. In both of the situations, the communities that gather might be local and from the same general community, but they are more ad hoc, unpredictable, and less bound together than a congregation would be. Still, awareness of the kinds of communal, cultural aspects outlined earlier can be helpful. What stories does a community tell about itself? Are there particular words or phrases that express communal identity or that insiders use? What symbols in and around the community are present and powerful, and how might they relate to the issue under consideration?

On the other hand, some communities that gather for public proclamation are more regular, even if the gathered community has some variation in those who attend. Take, for instance, two examples I have previously cited. The Poor People's Campaign has national and local gatherings and has been holding such events since its relaunch in 2017. Through this time, there are now those who would consider themselves to be regular participants or attenders. There are familiar rituals to these gatherings (even if they vary), habits of being together, stories about the groups that have developed and that are repeated, symbols, and language specific to the gatherings. For instance, knowing the role of music and communal singing built around the freedom song tradition could be helpful to a speaker in making their public proclamation coherent and consistent with the rest of the gathering.

Similarly, but on a more local level, the previously mentioned RISC congregation-based community organizing group meets in large gatherings two or three times a year. To point to one specific aspect of its developed culture, these gatherings feature a familiar, repeated, ritualized call-and-response chant in which a leader says, "Justice demands," and the people respond, "Risk!" This play on the group's name serves purposes of affirmation for something that has been said or done in the meeting, to call everyone to attention, and to bring unifying energy into the room. Knowing that RISC is multiracial, multiethnic (and multilingual via translators), and interfaith also provides information to the speaker that communication should be modulated in ways that speak with intercultural awareness and a generous sense of religious pluralism, even when a speaker claims distinctive aspects of their faith tradition. A speaker unaware of these cultural aspects might miss an opportunity to integrate their speaking within the culture frame of RISC. Community organizing groups often have such ways of being together when they gather.

The ecological and culture frames are separate ways of understanding, but closely related, with the ecological as a wider aperture and the cultural zooming in more closely. Being intentional about these two frames allows the speaker to speak in ways that might resonate more specifically with a community gathered for public proclamation.

The Resources Frame

The authors also suggest the critical importance of assessing the resources and perceptions of resources, as well as understanding the limits of those resources.[9]

> The resources frame is much simpler, asking a congregation what it has the "capital" to accomplish. . . . The "capital" to which you will give attention from this vantage point may be the congregation's members, its money, its buildings, its reputational and spiritual energies, its connections in the community, and even its history. These are the raw materials of congregational life. Some of them are hard and countable, such as money, people, and buildings; other resources are soft and elusive, such as shared experiences of hard times together or the strength of the faith and commitment of the congregation.[10]

This assessment includes what those resources are, to what purposes they can or will be put, and permission to tap into available resources. It is one thing to know about the resources a faith community has, but another entirely to know about how they perceive their resources as strengths or weaknesses, who controls the purse strings, and how people understand resources as they relate to congregational mission.

Regarding public proclamation, speakers can and should inventory the resources of the community that has gathered. As we have noted throughout, those resources differ based on the kind of community that gathers and the situation. In a previous chapter, I noted an interview between Milton West and the hosts of *Today* in the aftermath of devastating tornadoes in Mayfield, Kentucky, including the nearly complete destruction of the congregation's building. In describing the congregation and community, West says, "So we grieve and we cry and we hug and we pull ourselves together and go to the next

---

9. Ammerman et al., 15.
10. Ammerman et al., 15.

step of trying to recover . . . but our people have stayed strong during all of this." While we might think of the destruction as a complete loss of resources, West names the community's emotional, spiritual, and psychic resources that serve not just as reporting information about the community but also as an example for those who are watching the interview.

Later, in response to a question about how people who want to help can respond, West first suggests that people can respond with prayer, then identifies how they can give to the community or his congregation through financial donations online, and then pivots to name something different: "What I think is going to happen, to be frank with you, is I think our people are in an age where people are so fragmented and divided in their political, theological, and personal views . . . I think this gives people an opportunity to pull together for the common good. Those differences don't matter when you're trying to rebuild your lives. And so I think we're going to see that diminish here in Mayfield for quite some time."[11] By knowing the resource frame of both the Mayfield community and those who are watching the interview, West names prayer and financial gifts as resources that the devastated community needs. His pivot names a resource at work within the community that speaks to the larger common good: in this moment, people are turning away from differences and exercising goodwill toward one another beyond political, theological, and personal differences. The authors of *Studying Congregations* might call this a "soft and elusive" resource, but West has taken the opportunity to inventory it and subsequently name it as a resource that the community shares with one another and models to those who watch, knowing that this is a hidden resource in the current US context.

The resource frame allows speakers to name the goods and potential goods a community might use to achieve its strategic goals (see figure 1 on page 67). Thus, a critical question to answer is: What are the assets from which progress might be made? Those familiar with asset-based community development, which begins with identifying resources and strengths, rather than deficits, in a community, will undoubtedly see resonances here, especially as a starting place for organizing.[12] We might also think of this as a potential rhetorical strategy, particularly in communities that may feel defeated or hopeless or that are experiencing or have experienced loss. In terms of deficits and limits, this frame also

---

11. "Minister of Kentucky Church Talks Tornado Damage," December 13, 2021, YouTube, https://www.youtube.com/watch?v=P9B1DyB2lJs.

12. Pyles, *Progressive Community Organizing*, 224–26.

allows speakers to notice what holds a community back or, in conversation with the ecological and cultural frames, to know the forces that might restrict the resources a community possesses (or keeps it from possessing). Naming these purposefully within public proclamation empowers a community to recognize or reaffirm its strengths or to lift up its potential to achieve its strategic goals, and, in conversation with the next frame, to name what enables or is preventing the community from achieving its goals. The resource frame in public proclamation has tremendous potential to help build communal identity and a sense of capacity for what is possible.

The Process Frame

Fourth and finally, the process frame "calls attention to the underlying flow and dynamics of a congregation that knit together its common life and shape its morale and climate. Process perspectives ask how leadership is exercised and shared, how decisions are made, how communication occurs, and how conflicts are managed and problems are solved."[13] At first glance, this might seem like the least important frame for understanding the context and its relationship to instances of public proclamation. People do not gather to hear about process, but process does form a significant aspect of our understanding of context that should shape our speaking. I suggest that with public proclamation in view, we should consider two dimensions of the process frame.

The first dimension refers to the self in context, and particularly with respect to the processes that lead to our speaking. A quick accounting of where we are in terms of the organizational structure (if there is one), the relationships between speakers and the way in which we have arrived at the moment of speaking are critical. With these considerations in mind, we can clearly and accurately portray who we are and our place in the process when we speak. Of course, we do not want to dwell on this in our speaking, but even quick references can help give a sense of the process frame and offer transparency to those who are gathered. Speakers should inventory the following questions:

—How was I invited to speak?
—In what ways do I relate to leadership?
—Who else do I represent and how?
—To what extent do I represent that which is being advocated, articulated, or opposed?

13. Ammerman et al., *Studying Congregations*, 215–16.

—Are my identity and voice part of the majority and a privileged voice or are they minoritized in the context of the organization or presenting event?

As one example of the process frame, Terri Hord Owens, General Minister and President of the Christian Church (Disciples of Christ), spoke at the launch of the Poor People's Campaign, beginning her remarks this way:

> I am proud to stand here on behalf of the Christian Church (Disciples of Christ). We claim our brother Dr. [William J.] Barber as one of our own, but we stand here not just because of him but because of God and who God has called us to be. We are called to love God, but we can't do that unless we are also loving our neighbor as ourselves. This summer we passed a resolution at our General Assembly, which passed unanimously, saying that every level of the Christian Church (Disciples of Christ)—that includes congregations, our regional ministries, and our general ministries in the US and in Canada (there is much to be said about the systemic injustice that exist in Canada as well) —is to support this prophetic movement.[14]

A few things are going on here letting us know that Hord Owens understands the process frame. At the beginning, she acknowledges her status as a denominational representative. In a way that moves past formal process and organizational rhetoric, she also recognizes Barber's place as a minister within the denomination and goes so far as to use sibling language, acknowledging an allied connection and relationship beyond formal organizational ties (we might also note that this is language that is often deeply part of Black congregational life). She also makes two observations at the level of process about her denomination. First, she observes the resolution of the General Assembly of the Christian Church (Disciples of Christ), which voted to support the movement. Second, and within that statement, she also points to the reach of this resolution to congregations, regional ministries, and general ministries, both in the United States and Canada. These acknowledgments, integrated into her remarks, give a sense of the context from which she speaks. As such, she identifies a constituency on behalf of which she speaks and (ostensibly) to which she is speaking. And while her comments move toward more general applicability later on, acknowledging the process frame helps

---

14. "Poor, Disenfranchised, Clergy and Allies Launch Movement for Moral Revival in America," Repairers of the Breach, December 4, 2017, YouTube, https://www.youtube.com/watch?v=eyRdJjXO4wk.

establish her as part of the wide network that stands in support of the Poor People's Campaign agenda.

The second dimension has to do with how process relates to organizational actions. Speakers want to be clear about how they understand—and fit into—an organization's inner and external workings and, as a result, intentional about how their speaking portrays those organizational actions. Again, speakers need to be discerning about this, because people generally do not gather to hear about organizational process. Awareness helps present a coherent, consistent, and clear message that can also inform. This is especially helpful in first-time, emergency, or ad hoc gatherings, when information about process can be low for those who gather. In addition, although we might think it should go without saying, speakers need to know the process frame in order to know what the organization is going to do next and what people are asking. As such, speakers should inventory the following questions:

—What organizational processes are transparent in speaking, and to what extent do they need to be?
— What are the organization's next steps?
— What actions are those gathered being prepared or invited to take, and how do they relate to strategic goals?

Knowing the process frame helps speakers to convey how decisions are being made at the organizational level, which can portray an organization's stability and strength. In addition, it can be helpful to signal how the organization will proceed. For instance, a statement like, "Over the next week, we will sit down with city leaders to determine a path forward," can be helpful. Communicating what actions are desired is indispensable. In the same example, speakers can state that the gathering will be moving from a rally to a march, that the people are invited to write their elected representatives, or a host of other actions. Later in this chapter, we examine strategic goals. For now, we acknowledge that strategic actions exist within the process frame and are thus crucial in the kind of contextual inventory that prepares us for public proclamation.

These four frames help give us a sense of the lay of the land in which public proclamation participates. The wide view helps us situate our public proclamation within a broader context. While preparing with these frames in view might not naturally occur to us, it can be immensely valuable to attend to these dimensions of what prompts our speaking so that we can be clear, coherent, consistent, compelling, and as comprehensive as possible in our public proclamation.

Figure 1 shows these frames together in a Public Context Worksheet. It is also available in the appendix to copy and use when needed.

Figure 1

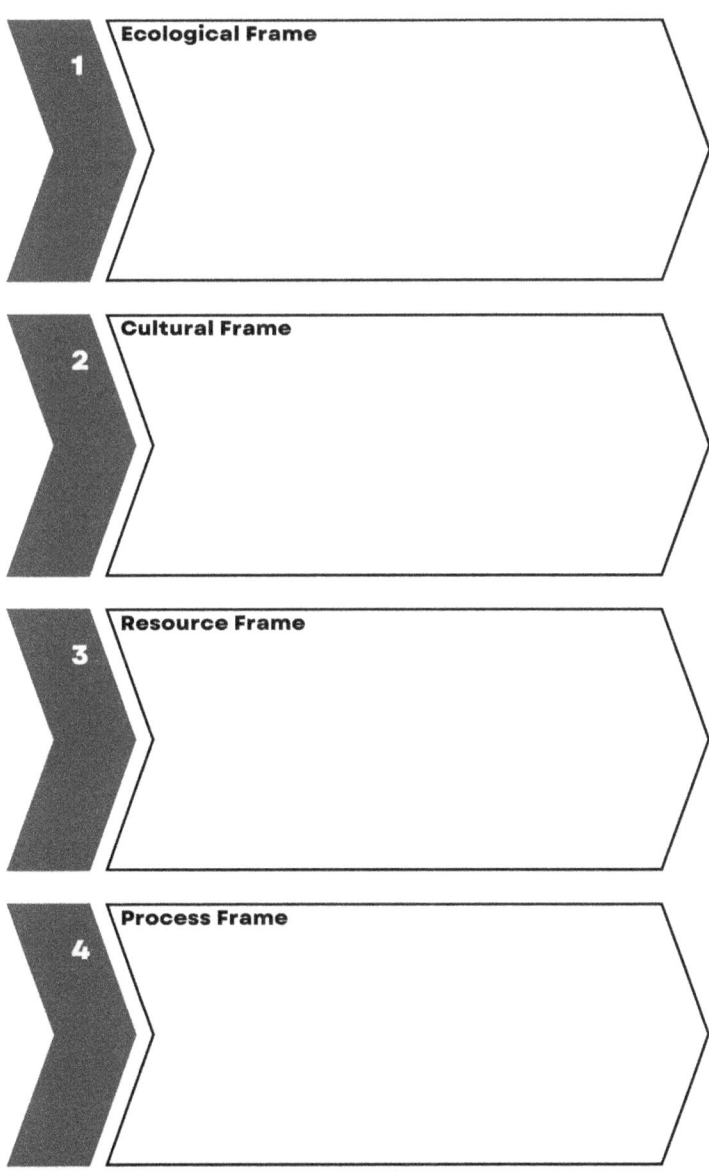

Public Context Worksheet: Wide View

Close View of Context

In addition to the wide view, it is also important to zoom in close to the situation that prompts public proclamation. Inasmuch as we pay attention to the broader context, we also need to pay attention to the in-the-moment contexts that might affect how we prepare for public proclamation or even how we might adjust extemporaneously. There will be some overlap with the wide view, but these close views help us to be specific when thinking through the finer details of the communicative event. I have placed these aspects of the close view into two categories of the gathering and the speaker.

Gathering

In terms of the gathering, we want to address the following questions:

—What is the medium for communication? Is it live and in person? Are still or video cameras involved? Is it a press conference that will be both live and recorded? An interview setting? An online gathering? Speakers should know about amplification as well.
—What is the location, what is its architecture, and how are people gathered? Gathering outside city hall with speakers on steps and a crowd gathered below is different from gathering in an enclosed civic space, such as the city council chambers. Gathering in a church, synagogue, or other religious space offers different dynamics. Knowing if there will be a podium, lectern, or other places to support microphones or notes will be important.
—What else will go on at the gathering? Will other speakers be there? Will there be singing, predetermined chants, prayers, or invitations to specific actions—symbolic or otherwise?
—What symbols will be shared, displayed, or created? Visual symbols can work in tandem with the spoken word to reinforce coherent, consistent, energizing, and unifying messages.

Speaker(s)

In terms of speakers, we want to understand who will speak and what dynamics they present. The following questions may be helpful:

—If there are other speakers, who are they? What is the order in which they will speak? Knowing if there are other speakers, how many, and the order in which they will speak helps us think about time, messaging, and appropriate similarities and differences between speeches. Diversity among speakers in terms of clergy or lay status, multiple or no faiths, as well as other aspects of social location can help determine what needs to be said from our own perspectives.

—How do speakers and listeners relate to each other in terms of prior relationship, authority, and physical proximity? In situations where we are known, we speak differently than in conditions when we are unknown or in which there is a mixture of prior relationship. Relationship can also be answered in part by the process frame. Those who are gathered might be heavily invested in the organizational framework, and that will shift a speaking situation from one in which those who are gathered are uninitiated. In some situations, Christian clergy carry a great deal of authority, while in others they may be respected to a lesser degree. The way our authority as clergy is or is not recognized is an important factor in what we say and how we carry ourselves. As noted earlier, physical proximity is also important.

—Somewhat related to the previous point, in what ways are speakers identified? Are clergy titles or other references used to identify how a speaker represents specific congregations or denominations? This also includes knowing how clergy are invited to dress—whether in plain dress, in clergy attire like collars or stoles, or with symbols representative of the organization or occasion.

To organize our analysis, the Public Context Worksheet: Close View (figure 2 on page 70) can be helpful.

STRATEGIC GOALS AND PUBLIC PROCLAMATION

Public Proclamation's Connection to Strategic Goals

Recall our working definition of public proclamation: "Public proclamation is communication that is intended for the public sphere, grounded in hope and employing faith-rooted language, with the purpose of working toward strategic goals of offering witness amid trouble, uniting in solidarity, and/or working toward justice and healing." The second major question in focus in the chapter is this: *"What is the strategic goal of the communicative situation?"*

Figure 2

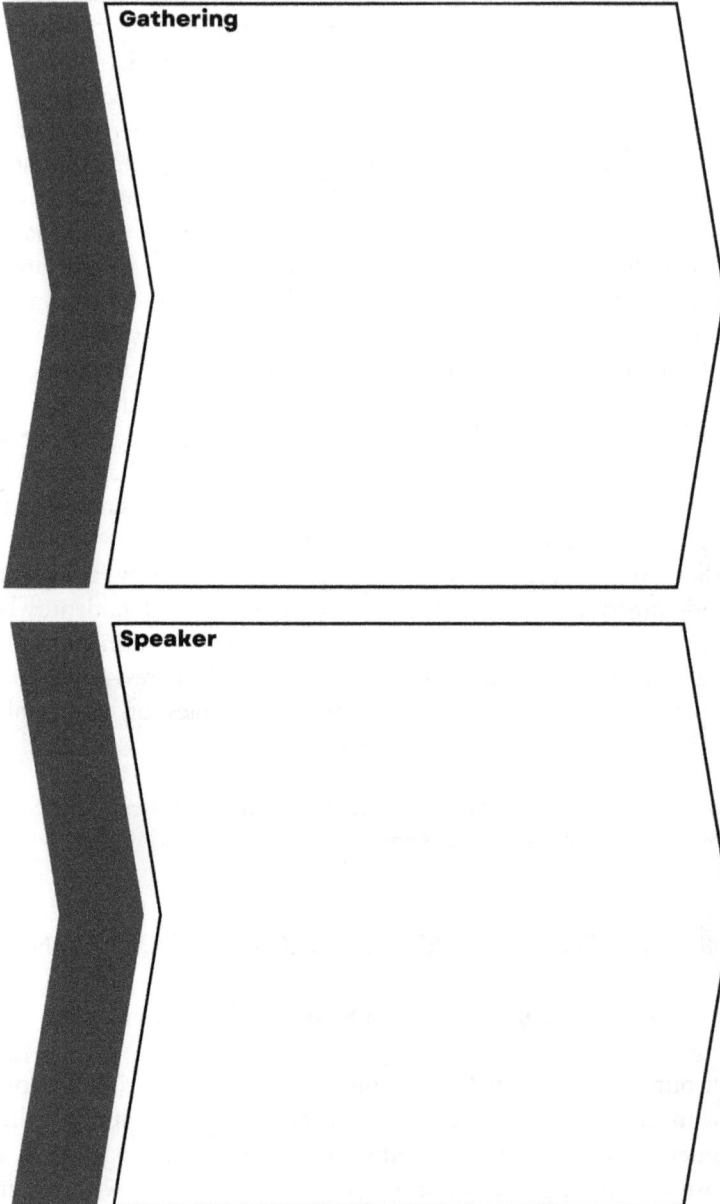

Public Context Worksheet: Close View

As we move toward shaping the message, this question encourages us to articulate what we hope will happen as a result of our speaking in a larger sense. In our working definition, I have offered some abstract goals rooted in our roles as faith leaders, but we have some more specific purposes for a speaking moment that fall under these broad goals (we explore these in the next chapter). Public proclamation should be anchored in the larger strategic goals of the moment, movement, or organization for which we are speaking. Thus, I want to differentiate between (1) how an instance of public proclamation connects to strategic goals and (2) what the purposes of an instance of public proclamation are. While different, they should work together.

In order to begin unpacking some of the possible strategic goals of our speaking and some methods for articulating this in connection to an instance of public proclamation, it is helpful first to have an understanding of what we mean by strategy and strategic goals. According to Loretta Pyles, "Strategy in organizing . . . is the sum total of the development of a vision; analysis of power; assessment of capacities; identification of issues and targets; and planning to achieve a goal."[15] Pyles contrasts this with the term "tactics," which "are specific actions and activities that are carried out to move toward a strategic goal."[16] This differentiation is important because with these terms before us, we are reminded that public proclamation is but one tactic within an overall strategy that moves toward goals. At the risk of being repetitive, I would suggest that this is important not only when connecting public proclamation to community organizing and long-term work but also when dealing with emergency moments that are disconnected from community organizing for social justice or that precede organization, such as situations that are in response to events, including natural disasters or community tragedy.

Pyles suggests that one way of working through strategy is with a "strategy chart," which "helps organizers dissect strategy into meaningful components."[17] The chart looks at five different categories:

1. Goals
2. Organizational considerations
3. Constituents, allies, and opponents
4. Targets
5. Tactics

15. Pyles, *Progressive Community Organizing*, 213.
16. Pyles, 213.
17. Pyles, 214.

While Pyles notes that this process is for organizing strategy, I suggest that these categories are also useful to consider in planning for instances of public proclamation.

As it relates to goals, once organizing groups have considered their focus issues and organizational process, Pyles encourages organizers to think through long-term, intermediate, and immediate goals. As a shorthand for those involved in public proclamation, we might begin to sketch out our planning notes for speaking with responses to two key questions: What do we want? When do we want it? Being specific about long-term, intermediate, and immediate goals of the organization will be helpful as we move forward. As noted earlier, in the next chapter, I encourage us to be even more specific about the purposes of the communicative event, which can help connect an instance of public proclamation to strategic goals.

Organizational considerations include thinking through the resources that groups invest in their campaigns. These may be important in terms of planning what we might ask of listeners. Will the effort need volunteers, money, or some other resources? In a different light, might these resources be something to lift up as a strength of the group?

Third are constituents, allies, and opponents. Here, Pyles suggests listing these out within the context of organizational planning. Who are the people that your work affects? Who are the current and potential allies? Who opposes your work? Naming these people and groups helps us be more specific in thinking through who we are addressing and how we address them. The fourth element is thinking through who the targets are of particular actions (a particular politician or community leader? a group of supporters?).

The fifth element is more directed toward an organizational plan and perhaps less helpful in planning public proclamation: the tactics or activities in which the group will engage (as noted earlier, public proclamation is one such tactic).[18] Still, it may be helpful to list the sphere of actions in which public proclamation may be involved and certainly to be able to connect one's public proclamation to the wider set of tactics when useful.

To summarize important components of the strategy chart in preparing for public proclamation, we want to take time to consider the following:

—*Goals*: What do we want? When do we want it?
—*Organizational considerations*: What are our resources? What do we need?

---

18. Pyles, 214.

—*People*
- Constituents: Who is impacted?
- Allies (or would-be allies): Who is or might be with us?
- Opponents: Who opposes us?

—*Targets*: To whom is this instance of public proclamation directed?
—*Tactics, other than public proclamation*: These might include such things as demonstrations/rallies/protests, organizing meetings, meetings with public officials, resource drives (money, membership, goods), one-on-one meetings (door-to-door) and phone calls, crafting policy and position statements, social media outreach, and the like.

We could visualize the chart as shown in figure 3 on page 74.

Examples of Strategic Goals in Public Proclamation

To flesh out what strategic goals in public proclamation look like, I want to trace through a few examples, using some of the scenarios I have already reviewed. First, let's look at Milton West's interview with *Today* after the tornadoes that destroyed much of Mayfield, Kentucky. At first glance, this scenario might not lend itself well to an example of strategic goals. West does not connect his responses to the strategic goals of a movement or community organizing group. He represents no one other than his congregation and, to some degree, the community at large. West's invitation to interview might be more about the shocking visual of the undamaged communion table in the midst of an almost completely destroyed church sanctuary and town. And although we might identify a few purposes in his responses (again, we look at this more in the next chapter), it might be difficult to detect a connective thread that points to a strategic goal. Still, in answering the questions "What do we want? When do we want it?" I suggest that West seizes the opportunity to bear public witness to the nature of the church in society. Underlying West's responses, he understands that many have well-founded doubts about the church, its theological commitments, and its role in society. West's responses articulate a witness to the nature of the church by portraying a church that seeks the civic good and theology that frames a healthy understanding of God's role in natural disasters.

Second, consider the 2017 relaunch of the Poor People's Campaign. Again, while there are many purposes to the short speeches at the launch,

Figure 3

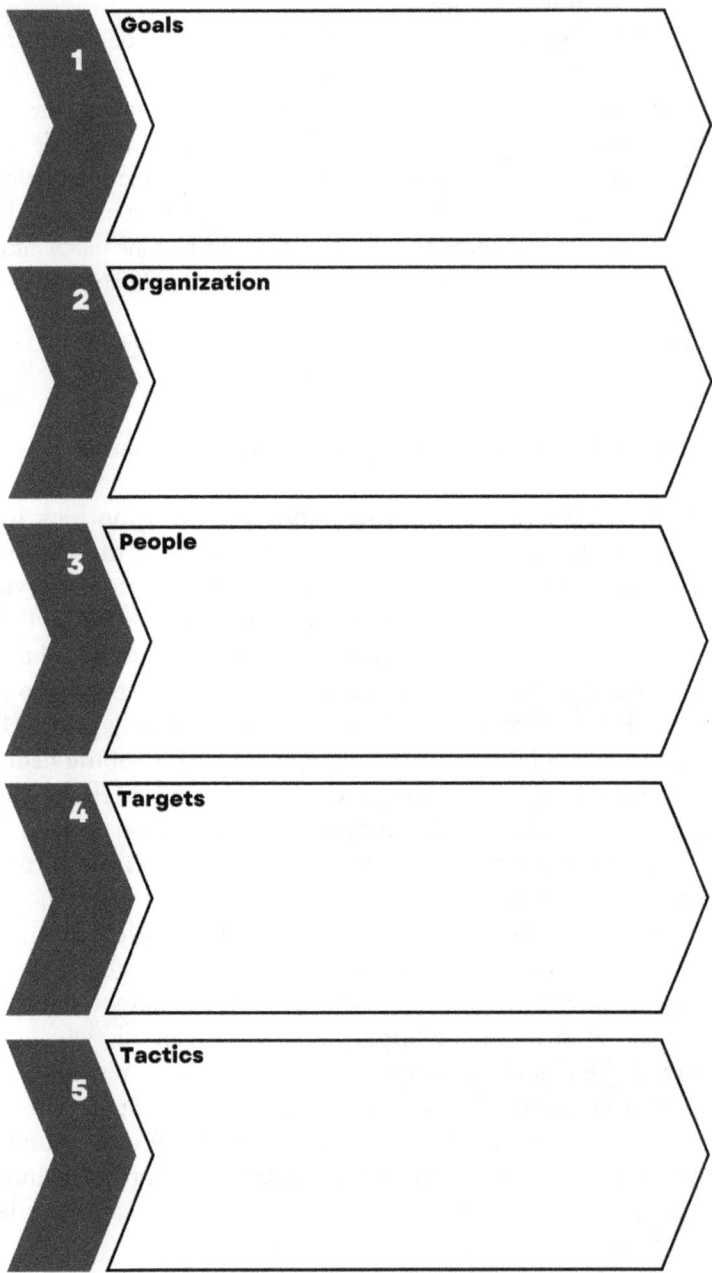

Strategic Goals Worksheet

only one of which I detailed earlier, I would suggest that all the speeches relate to and reinforce the strategic goals of the Poor People's Campaign. In summary, the Poor People's Campaign identifies its strategic goals in the following way:

We rise together because:

1. We rise to demand that the 140 million poor and low-income people in our nation—from every race, creed, color, sexuality and place—are no longer ignored, dismissed or pushed to the margins of our political and social agenda.
2. We rise not as left or right, Democrat or Republican, but as a moral fusion movement to build power, build moral activism, build voter participation, and we won't be silent anymore!
3. We rise to change the moral narrative and demand that the interlocking injustices of systemic racism, poverty, ecological devastation, the war economy/militarism and the distorted moral narrative of religious nationalism all be ended.
4. We rise to challenge the lie of scarcity in the midst of abundance.
5. We rise to lift the voices and faces of poor and low-income Americans and their moral allies with a new vision of love, justice, and truth for America that says poverty can be abolished and change can come.[19]

At the press conference that launched the campaign, those who gathered and spoke came from the ranks of religious leaders across Christian denominations and faith traditions, civic leaders, those who identify as poor and low-income, as well as leaders of various labor unions, all from diverse social locations. In their speaking, each person pointed to (and participated in) the strategic goals outlined here. As it relates to faith leaders' public proclamation, note the key words: "together," "every . . . creed," "moral fusion movement," "moral activism," "distorted moral narrative of religious nationalism," and "moral allies." When faith leaders like Hord Owens rose to speak, they did so to identify themselves as part of a unified coalition to accomplish these goals.

Third and finally, I want to highlight a brief speech from a RISC leader. In August 2023, RISC held a rally outside city hall in Richmond as its leaders met with Mayor Levar Stoney, imploring him to implement a

---

19. Poor People's Campaign, "About," accessed July 24, 2024, https://www.poorpeoplescampaign.org/about/.

program called Group Violence Intervention (GVI), which RISC identified as an evidence-based program that could help move toward one of its two strategic goals: ending gun violence in Richmond. In that meeting, Mayor Stoney communicated that he would not implement GVI. RISC interfaith members and leaders, as well as other allies, had gathered before the meeting to state the purpose of its gathering, to sing, and to pray. RISC members stayed at the entrance to city hall throughout the meeting, continuing in song and prayer. When the meeting with the mayor was over, RISC leaders communicated with several purposes but pointing to the strategic goal. Pastor Don Coleman rose to the podium and said,

> Yes, it was discouraging but we are not discouraged. We will continue to press to what will make a difference. We will continue to press that if we work together something can happen to change this gun violence, so we're going to move forward. We're going to move forward because we outlast every elected official. Clap your hands! We outlast every one of them. And we put future mayoral candidates on notice. We are here and we will be pushing for GVI and as a matter of fact, I'll say it this way: if you want to get elected mayor of Richmond, you better get with us![20]

Note as well here how Coleman identifies organizational considerations (effort, determination, and political power) and targets (future mayoral candidates).

CONCLUSION

In this chapter, I have identified the importance of knowing the context and identifying the strategic goals for speaking. When we take these preparatory steps, we gain a better sense of how our instances of public proclamation work out of and fit into the larger landscape of our communities, and we are better able to see our public proclamation as integral to the strategic goals of the organization, movement, or moment in which we are called to speak. The worksheet in figure 3 (p. 74) and in the appendix put these considerations into a form that can help in the planning process for public proclamation.

---

20. "RISC's Response to Mayor Stoney's Rejection of Program," *Richmond-Times Dispatch*, August 29, 2023, YouTube, https://www.youtube.com/watch?v=ySMvtW_FZgM.

As we move into the next chapter, we also move closer into the elements that can help us form what we want to say in the public square.

EXERCISE YOUR VOICE

Think through either a previous instance of public proclamation, a gathering where you are planning to speak, or a scenario for which you would speak. Fill out the Public Context Worksheet: Wide View, Public Context Worksheet: Close View, and the Strategic Goals Worksheet to think through the contexts and strategic goals of your chosen instance of public proclamation. These worksheets are included in the appendix so that they can be used for other instances of public proclamation.

4
Knowing What to Speak in the Public Square

Now that we have thought deeply about who we are, the contexts in which we will speak, and the strategic goals that public proclamation serves, it is time to get specific about what we will say. As we make our way through this chapter, I'll invite us into practices that can help us answer the questions *What are the theological emphases needed for this communicative situation, what is it that I want to say, and how do I hope people will respond?* As we ourselves explore ways to respond and prepare for public proclamation, we will again identify some tools that are familiar for sermon preparation but adjusted for different purposes in the public square.

THE NATURE OF THEOLOGICAL CLAIMS IN PUBLIC PROCLAMATION: FAITH-ROOTED SPEECH

Before we dive into these practices, I want us to consider again my definition of public proclamation:

> Public proclamation is communication that is intended for the public sphere, grounded in hope and employing faith-rooted language, with the purpose of working toward strategic goals of offering witness amid trouble, uniting in solidarity, and/or working toward justice and healing.

When faith leaders step into the public square to speak, we must wrestle with the question *How do I speak with integrity from a faith perspective in a pluralistic gathering and one in which some might be antagonistic to Christian faith?* The idea of faith-rooted language, as I suggested in the introduction, is a particular way of framing faith ideas, practices, and commitments. Faith-rooted language plays a critical role when we do the work of public proclamation. However, this is not the kind of speech that we are used to in our insulated faith communities when we gather for worship. Or, I should say, it typically isn't that. On the other hand, we represent faith traditions and communities of belief and practice when we speak in public. And while simply discharging ourselves of faith-y language might be easy when we come into the public sphere, I believe we do ourselves and our communities a disservice if we fully abandon faith language. We need to find ways of owning and expressing our faith commitments that are authentic and genuine for us, as well as accessible to people of all or no faith traditions.[1]

As I noted in the introduction, I am borrowing the term "faith-rooted" from Alexia Salvatierra and Peter Heltzel, who advocate for "faith-rooted organizing" as different in substance from "faith-based organizing."[2] It does not serve our purposes to trace the differences between those models of community organizing here. The authors are careful to say that "faith-rooted organizing comprehensively and carefully examines all that faith brings to the table of change—from visions and dreams, to values, to scriptures and sacred texts, to symbols and rituals. . . . Faith-rooted organizing is designed to enable the faith 'sector' to give its best to the whole."[3]

As we turn our attention to the kind of language we use in the public square as faith leaders, Salvatierra and Heltzel's words provide a helpful start, because it means that we need not shirk away from our faith commitments in the public square. In fact, our faith allows us to give our "best to the whole." Still, to what degree do we use faith language? While Salvatierra and Heltzel give permission in their

---

1. John McClure calls this "the theosymbolic code" in Christian sermons. This is a feature that shifts when we think about practices that migrate from the pulpit to the public square. Public proclamation's theological meaning-making will be present but often in much different ways than in the Christian sermon. See John S. McClure, *The Four Codes of Preaching: Rhetorical Strategies* (Westminster John Knox, 2004), 93–135.

2. Alexia Salvatierra and Peter Heltzel, *Faith-Rooted Organizing: Mobilizing the Church in Service to the World* (InterVarsity, 2013), 9–13.

3. Salvatierra and Heltzel, 10.

broad detailing of organizing strategy, they do not help us discern the more specific ways that our faith commitments might show up in public proclamation. Here I think the metaphor they deploy in "faith-rooted" is especially helpful, even if unexplored in their work.[4] The idea of "rootedness" gives us an agricultural metaphor worth exploring regarding the language of public proclamation. Rootedness allows us some options and a kind of continuum for the degree to which faith language emerges in public proclamation.

For some situations, a faith leader might choose to be less overt and more suggestive in their references to faith as they speak. In this instance, we might think of rootedness being like an onion, carrot, peanut, or potato. While there is a plant that shows above ground and indeed the stem and leaves that show can help identify what is growing, the roots and what is substantively growing remain underground. In this way, faith-rooted speech is the kind of speech that is significantly informed and shaped by faith, but public proclamation need not prominently feature the symbols and vocabulary of faith. This approach can be especially useful in settings with a pluralistic and widely diverse audience and one in which many people might feel antagonistic to faith or in situations in which the symbols and vocabulary of faith might not be well known or hold wide appeal.

For other situations, a faith leader might be more moderate in their use of the symbols and vocabulary of faith. Here we might think of rootedness being like strawberry plants, lettuce, cabbage, or soybeans. If you have ever picked strawberries, you know that they grow close to the ground, not far from their roots. The plants do not grow tall or put on a great flowering display. In this model, I think of the strawberry plant as a moderate way of envisioning faith-rooted speech. In this place on the continuum, faith leaders might use the words of Scripture, symbols of faith, and language of the Divine, but with some restraint. This can be useful in settings where faith language has some cache or in which a diverse audience would be open to the ways that faith informs thinking about whatever has precipitated the gathering. In addition, it can be helpful in settings where multiple faiths are represented as speakers or listeners, and we want to show how our unique faith expressions share commonalities that can unite us toward the strategic goals for which we're gathered.

---

4. Here I want to credit former student Stacy Deyerle for first beginning to tease out the helpfulness of this metaphor for public proclamation.

On the far opposite end of the continuum would be something like a cherry tree. Unlike the potato/carrot/onion or the low-growing strawberry/lettuce/soybean, the cherry tree not only grows tall away from its roots but also grows significant blooms and flowers before it bears fruit. Even from a distance, many can recognize the tall, flowering cherry tree. Here faith-rooted speech is overt. The symbols and vocabulary of faith, as well as Scripture references and naming of the Divine, are prominent. This approach can be especially useful in settings where we might need to justify our involvement as people of faith or in settings where clarity around ideas or practices based in faith is warranted. It might also be useful in settings with a preponderance of Christians in attendance.

The continuum I have outlined here is just that, and I am confident that there are situations in which faith leaders will want to move across the continuum depending on the context, strategic goals, the presence of other faith leaders, and the listeners who have gathered. The way we practice faith-rooted speech need not be limited to a singular approach in every situation. With this in mind, we now turn to thinking more specifically about the theological claims from which our public proclamation will operate.

THEOLOGICAL CLAIMS: IDENTIFYING WHAT GOD IS UP TO AND WHY

Having established some guidelines for what faith-rooted speech might mean for us, I want us to think seriously about how our theological claims undergird our speaking, no matter where we might fall along the continuum. As faith leaders, being clear about the theological justifications for whatever we might be saying helps ground us. Otherwise, we run the risk of inconsistency or lack of coherence in our messaging—or we might fall into the trap of grounding our rationale solely in whatever political ideology is driving us, distancing us from the faith communities and commitments we represent. Again, I invite you to remember that even with strong theological claims, we need not be overt about them in every single instance. That said, we should be clear about how our theological commitments are informing us, no matter where we land on the continuum.

To help us do this, I want to borrow a practice from homiletics. First, a quick distinction: There is a difference between theology *of* preaching and theology *for* (alternatively: *in, and*) preaching. The former refers to thinking theologically about the practice of preaching and conceptualizing a theological framework for what happens in the preparation, embodiment, and communal engagement of sermons. As a parallel, this is what we were discussing in chapter 1 as we explored different theological frameworks for thinking about public proclamation. What we are engaged in here is similar to theology *for* preaching, that is, considering the kinds of theological claims that inform the content of what we will say.[5]

As a way of becoming clearer about theological claims in sermons, homiletician Paul Scott Wilson encourages preachers to "choose one doctrine" for their sermons. As he notes, "A doctrine is a teaching of the church on a topic. Some students are intimidated by the word "doctrine"; they think they do not know enough about theology and get stressed. One teacher, Sam Persons Parkes, tells them to relax, calm down, and be clear, 'The doctrine is what I am claiming about God.'"[6] As we orient ourselves toward theological claims, I am not suggesting (nor is Wilson) that public proclamation should become a treatise on a particular aspect of systematic theology. Remember that we are engaging in communicative public theology, and it is important to recognize that as we explore a theological claim for an instance of public proclamation, it "may have a direct, obvious impact . . . or it may simply clarify and deepen [our] thought."[7]

Wilson's focus on doctrinal statements points us in a good general direction, encouraging us to think more deliberatively about how theology impacts our speaking. In working toward identifying theological claims for sermons, I find homiletician Leah Schade's approach to be helpful. According to Schade, Sumney, and Askew, "Theological Claims in Scripture and sermons are assertions about the nature of God and God's work in the world. Further, assertions about the nature and work of Jesus Christ and the nature and work of the Holy Spirit are also Theological Claims."[8] They go on to distinguish theological claims from two other types of claims: anthropological claims, which "make claims about who human beings are as creations of God and, as such, what we

---

5. See, for instance, John S. McClure, *Preaching Words: 144 Key Terms in Homiletics* (Westminster John Knox, 2007), 136–40.

6. Paul Scott Wilson, *The Four Pages of the Sermon: A Guide to Biblical Preaching*, rev. and updated ed. (Abingdon, 2018), 48–49.

7. Wilson, 49.

8. Leah D. Schade, Jerry L. Sumney, and Emily Askew, *Introduction to Preaching: Scripture, Theology, and Sermon Preparation* (Rowman and Littlefield, 2023), 93.

are to believe or do," and ecclesiological claims, which "have as their subject the church and are usually related to the growth or nature of the church as it instantiates the body of Christ."[9] While the authors encourage preachers to avoid these claims in their preaching preparation, I suggest a looser approach, especially for public proclamation, even though I would suggest that most of our claims will be theological claims in the sense that she suggests. The point is to be clear about what we actually believe theologically and how it connects to what we want to say and, as the authors note, to avoid theological cliches that "may be familiar and popular, [but] can be hollow and unhelpful at best, harmful at worst."[10] The caution against cliches is particularly important in the public square since we find ourselves in an age in which many people in public find trite theological language indicative of the church's shallowness, uselessness, or complicity in harm.

For sermons, we normally want theological claims to arise from the biblical text(s) under consideration. That is to say, our exegetical work on biblical texts should lead to theological claims. However, public proclamation does not work that way. People preparing for public proclamation are typically not going to engage in the kind of exegetical work that happens for weekly sermon preparation; time and circumstance typically prevent us from doing so. Even more, when we prepare for public proclamation, we might or might not prioritize a biblical text as the foundation. This can come as a significant shift.[11] Those of us who operate with the assumption that "biblical preaching is the *normative* form of Christian preaching," as Tom Long suggests, might feel that something is missing.[12] As Long goes on to note, "The kind of preaching that involves sermons that engage particular texts in the Bible is normative first of all because it reenacts the epistemology of the church, or put more simply, it models the primary way in which the church comes to know God's will."[13] Long makes a significant claim here: weekly use of the Bible in preaching forms the church's way of knowing. This is a powerful force that shapes us. However, in public proclamation, we are likely not operating in the same linear fashion of exegesis to sermon.

9. Schade, Sumney, and Askew, 103.
10. Schade, Sumney, and Askew, 98.
11. Again, here is a difference from the Christian sermon. What McClure calls "the Scriptural code" is often absent and certainly is not a central component or partner in public proclamation in the way that it is for the Christian sermon. See McClure, *The Four Codes of Preaching*, 15–51.
12. Thomas G. Long, *The Witness of Preaching*, 3rd ed. (Westminster John Knox, 2016), 59.
13. Long, 61.

Having said this, we can still operate from biblical texts as a central part of our preparation or in the content of what we say, and perhaps we will. Many biblical texts can support us in the wide variety of situations to which we may be called to speak, and our context may warrant our prioritization of a biblical text. But even when this is the case, I want to acknowledge that our preparation for public proclamation will not mirror an exegetical process for preaching preparation. I would suggest that, as a result, identifying our theological claims is all the more important.

Since we are not likely undertaking an exegetical process and are not working toward a sermon for a congregation, the theological claim will look a bit different than what Schade, Sumney, and Askew prescribe. Still, the theological claim should be *one sentence* that expresses a clear, coherent theological assertion that comes from significant conversation between our contextual analysis and the resources of theological reflection: Scripture, tradition, reason, and experience. For instance, in a sermon based on Genesis 32:22–32 (Jacob wrestling the angel at the Jabbok), the authors suggests that a theological claim should be formulated this way: "God's wrestling with Jacob resulted in both pain and blessing, transforming him in the process, as symbolized by his new name—Israel." They advise that the theological claim should make deep connections to the biblical text. Since our purposes are different, we want to take an approach that is less connected to a biblical text and may seem a little more abstract. The authors offer another possibility that points us in a better direction: "God sometimes struggles with humans, and that struggle often changes them."[14] While this statement works from an exegetical process and for a sermon for a particular congregational context, not for an instance of public proclamation, notice how their claim clearly states something about the action of God. Our theological claims should do the same in terms of format, whether we are saying something about God, Jesus, or the Holy Spirit. Let's take a look at some possible categories and examples.

Four Types of Theological Claims for Public Proclamation

Taking our cue from Schade, Sumney, and Askew that theological claims are assertions about the nature and action of God, Jesus Christ, or the Holy Spirit in the world, I propose at least four types of theological claims we might make in public proclamation: theological judgment, theological

---

14. Schade, Sumney, and Askew, *Introduction to Preaching*, 111.

warrant for action, theological explanation of the situation (reframing counterwitness), and theological permission-giving. I will explore each of these in detail below.

Theological Judgment

Our first category seeks to offer judgment in a strong theological grounding. Especially important for times of protest, theological judgment helps us make strong faith claims that can help people find the language and reasoning for opposition or support. For instance, as I write this chapter, the United States has experienced another shooting of a Black woman in her home: Sonya Massey, who was also known to have struggled with mental illness.[15]

For an instance of public proclamation, we could ground our speaking in a simple opposition to police violence based on the idea that police are meant to serve and protect citizens, the statistics around elevated police violence toward people of color, or policing as it relates to those struggling with mental health. These issues are important and not to be minimized or overlooked. As faith leaders seeking to do the work of communicative public theology, however, I would suggest that we might add to the public conversation through a more explicit theological framework. In this case, a possibility might be as follows: "God's love for all people makes a way for peace and nonviolence, and actions of violence, especially against marginalized and defenseless people, oppose God's ways in the world." A faith leader putting forth this perspective could offer strong judgment against this instance, as well as all instances and forms, of police violence. Again, as noted earlier, this theological claim is grounded in the nature of God, and the claim is rooted in theological foundations of Scripture, tradition, reason, and experience.

Theological Warrant for Action

Second, we might want to offer a theological justification for people to act. This theological warrant can be helpful when we are working to mobilize others to take action. While appeals to civic-mindedness or democratic principles are important, I want to emphasize again the importance of faith leaders adding their voices and rationale to the mix.

For instance, in revisiting Terri Hord Owens's speech to help launch the Poor People's Campaign, she said, "We stand here because

---

15. "With DUI-Related Ejection from Army, Deputy Who Killed Massey Should Have Raised Flags, Experts Say," AP News, July 29, 2024, https://apnews.com/article/massey-911-deputy-shooting-springfield-6ac3ff78bc29f18bd65c6e2763fab96f.

of God and who God has called us to be. We are called to love God, but we can't do that unless we are also loving our neighbor as ourselves."[16] In seeking to invite others to join the work of the Poor People's Campaign, Hord Owens grounds her appeal through a theological claim based on Matthew 22:37–39. We might slightly reframe what she says to make the theological claim one simple sentence: "God calls us to express our love of God through love of neighbor." In this instance, the theological claim is grounded in Scripture and clearly expresses something about God's nature and action through the words of Jesus.

Theological Explanation of the Situation (Reframing, Counterwitness)

Our third category is that of offering a theological explanation, reframing, or counterwitness of the situation. This kind of theological claim can be helpful when there are multiple theological interpretations of a situation that are confusing or conflicting. Such explanations or attempts to reframe can bring clarity and strong witness to the public and can offer faith perspectives as a way of bringing understanding to those who have gathered.

An excellent example of this is Milton West's interview on *Today*. When one of the interviewers asked West how the congregation was doing and followed up about the still-standing communion table amid the tornadic destruction, West took the opportunity to move the conversation in a different direction, saying, "What you try to do is to have them reframe, rethink what it all means and not to overinterpret it. You know there are a lot of people out there who would say that this is a sign from God that something is wrong. We do not embrace that notion at all. Our faith is positive, and God is never the author of bad things in people's lives."[17] West knows of multiple, conflicting, and harmful theological interpretations of the tornados in his community—and other natural disasters in the United States, most prominently in responses to Hurricane Katrina—so he takes the opportunity to offer a theological explanation (and for some listeners, a reframing) that can offer clarity amid confusion and an interpretation that can help prevent harm toward others. While the interview explores several different avenues, we might say that this portion is supported by the embedded theological claim: "God is never the author of bad things in people's lives."

---

16. "Poor, Disenfranchised, Clergy and Allies Launch Movement for Moral Revival in America," Repairers of the Breach, December 4, 2017, YouTube, https://www.youtube.com/watch?v=eyRdJjXO4wk.

17. "Minister of Kentucky Church Talks Tornado Damage," December 13, 2021, YouTube, https://www.youtube.com/watch?v=P9B1DyB2lJs.

Theological Permission-Giving

The fourth category might well be one that we could classify in the area of pastoral theology. Sometimes public proclamation takes place amid confusing, difficult, or traumatic events. In such moments, people might need permission to feel and express emotions that they often try to hide, and having theological justification for expressing the range of human emotions can be especially helpful. Whether that is anger, grief, or joy, theological permission-giving can be a helpful public pastoral work.

For instance, I often ask students to imagine their role as faith leaders heading up vigils in their communities after mass shootings. While the topic is unpleasant, I want them to be able to imagine one possibility of the kind of public and ritual environments they may encounter in their ministries. This kind of instance for public proclamation might lead us to a theological claim such as, "Because God grieves over every life taken and is angered by unjust, inhumane actions, we, too, can grieve and be angry." We do not have to go far in Scripture or theological traditions to see warrant for this claim. Now we might see this as a possible reframe or explanation, and some overlap may be present here, but I do not see the need for firm distinctions among these types. In this instance, however, the theological claim explicitly offers permission for people to experience and express emotions that they might otherwise try to suppress, particularly in instances where there is a quick push toward forgiveness or moving forward.

In planning and preparing for public proclamation, I encourage us to examine our beliefs carefully and then be explicit about our theological claims. This type of public theology helps set the record straight about who we are, what we believe, and why we are engaged in the public sphere, and it can also help tremendously those who are gathered. Ongoing biblical study, theological reflection, exploration of Christian history, and reflection on experience can aid us in speaking messages in the public sphere that represent generous and life-giving faith perspectives. As we continue our planning and preparation process, identifying the theological claim is an indispensable step along the way.

CENTRAL CLAIM: IDENTIFYING WHAT YOUR PUBLIC PROCLAMATION IS SAYING

Remember the second half of our prompting question for this chapter: *"What are the theological emphases needed for this communicative situation and what is it that I want to say?"* When we put together our contextual analysis of the communicative situation and our theological claim, we are moving toward a statement that can provide clarity and coherence for our public proclamation.

There are significant parallels here to any number of introductory preaching textbooks. In discussing sermon preparation, many authors suggest different names for this statement: the focus statement, the sermon summary sentence, the big idea, the theme statement, the good news statement, or the sermon in a sentence; these are just a few examples. The wisdom here is simple: One sentence can distill what we want to say so that a sermon can be clear, unified, coherent, and consistent. How many of us have heard (or preached!) sermons that were several sermons in one or that veered off course to follow rabbit trails? Chances are that either the preacher did not put in the work to identify a single, specific sentence—or they did, but did not allow that sentence to guide the sermon from beginning to end. This sentence acts as a grounding and centering force for the sermon. As I often say to students, this sentence is what we would desperately hope to hear in the handshake line after worship if, when people said, "Good sermon, Pastor," we simply asked, "Oh, thank you! What was the sermon about?"

As we move toward adapting this practice for public proclamation, I again want to pick up Schade, Sumney, and Askew's way of framing this practice. They call this statement the "central claim," which they define as "the primary assertion of the sermon—in *one* sentence. Think of it as writing a one-sentence summary to convey the essence of your message."[18] What sets these authors' version apart is the sort of formula they use to help write the central claim. For Schade, Sumney, and Askew, a type of mathematical formula is at work: *theological claim + central question = central claim*.[19] We have already reviewed the theological claim. The central question is a result of the exegetical process and contextual analysis, putting together the questions a biblical text seems to raise that parallel the questions arising from and in the congregational context.

Since we are not conducting biblical exegesis for a sermon, the central question is not now a factor for us. However, we do already have materials that mirror the role of the central question. We have a precipitating event or moment that calls us to speak and some contextual

---

18. Schade, Sumney, and Askew, *Introduction to Preaching*, 161.
19. Schade, Sumney, and Askew, 156.

analysis that has clarified what is going on and why. For our purposes, let's use the term "critical context" in place of "central question." I have chosen the word "critical" for two purposes: I want to imply (1) that there is some immediacy, or what we might alternatively call a precipitating event, that necessitates our speaking, and (2) that we have done some critical analysis about the precipitating event, the context in which we will speak. To borrow and revise the authors' mathematical formula: *theological claim + critical context = central claim.* When we work toward writing our central claim, we need to attend to how these elements come together.

Before offering a few examples, I want to follow Schade, Sumney, and Askew's lead in pointing out what the central claim is not. As with sermons, so, too, with the central claim for public proclamation: it is not a vague or general theological theme that fails to address specific aspects of the context. Nor is it merely a general assessment of the context without a theological frame. Second, the central claim is not a paragraph or lengthy explanation. Remember that the central claim should be one sentence. Don't get cute or overcomplicated here. The purpose is to provide one sentence that helps the instance of public proclamation be clear, coherent, consistent, and unified. In addition, if we are speaking extemporaneously or just from notes rather than a manuscript, the central claim can be a device that draws us back if we are tempted to stray. If the central claim is overly complicated, we risk losing or confusing those who have gathered. Third, just as for sermons, the central claim is not just a title for the speech. While few of us need titles for public proclamation in the same way that we might for a sermon, the same idea is at play here. Even more for our purposes, nor is the central claim a simple refrain or catchphrase that we might repeat in our speaking.

Let's work toward just a couple of examples of what the central claim for public proclamation might look like. To do this, I want to build on the examples I raised earlier with the different types of theological claims. These examples are flexible, and you might think about how you would alter them if you were planning to speak on these occasions. Remember, however, our formula for the central claim with public proclamation in mind: *theological claim + critical context = central claim.*

First, we take up the police murder of Sonya Massey in Illinois. The theological claim was this: "God's love for all people makes a way for peace, justice, and nonviolence, and actions of violence, especially against marginalized and defenseless people, oppose God's ways in the world." Let's imagine that we are addressing the city council of Springfield, Illinois, along with leaders across the community who represent multiple Christian denominations and other faith traditions. We know the continuing stories of lethal police force against people of color and those experiencing mental health crises across the United States. We know that the police officer who fired against Massey had a history of misconduct. So, we have this immediate situation, a pattern of situations like it, and some indications that the system of hiring qualified individuals to conduct community policing can be highly flawed. If we were members of this community, we may know other details closer to the ground, as well as more details that would point to a larger strategic goal, perhaps something like community pressure to reform police hiring, training, and discipline in Springfield.

Our central claim might be something like the following: "Because God's love for all people makes a way for peace, justice, and nonviolence, we condemn the police murder of Sonya Massey as an affront to God's ways in the world." Of course, there is more to say and much more to unpack. We need not worry about that at this stage. What we have here is a statement that helps us work toward a clear, consistent, and unified message with solid theological footing.

Second, consider the message of Hord Owens at the launch of the Poor People's Campaign. The theological claim was this: "God calls us to express our love of God through love of neighbor." In terms of critical context, recall that this speech was part of a press conference that included representatives from multiple denominations, labor organizations, and other social service organizations. A press conference means a more general audience, but we know that, in this case, other faith leaders, laypeople, elected officials, and members of labor and other social service organizations are part of the intended audience. There is a historical aspect to the critical context, as the Poor People's Campaign picks up the legacy of the original Poor People's Campaign in 1968 and has the strategic goal of mobilizing voters to work collectively toward the interest of those who are caught in interlocking, systemic inequalities of poverty and racism, as well as holding elected officials accountable for legislation, especially around the areas of militarism and ecological devastation. Since the speech has already been given, we are moving backward as we formulate the central claim. Our central claim might be something like: "God's imperative that loving our neighbor is love of God requires us to collectively seek the good of those who are impoverished by political, economic, and social systems."

These are just two examples of central claims drawn from the four scenarios I offered in the section on theological claims. You might try to develop central claims for the other two, though the interview with Milton West will be a little more difficult, since he is being interviewed and seems to be agreeable with the interview moving in multiple directions. In this case, I would say that the central claim would be quite general.

CENTRAL PURPOSE: IDENTIFYING WHAT DRIVES YOUR PUBLIC PROCLAMATION

As a third element in this aspect of preparation, we should be specific about the purpose of our speaking. In answering the question "What is the strategic goal of the communicative situation?" we have focused thus far on how an instance of public proclamation is connected to the larger goals of an organization, movement, or precipitating event. We have also focused on how public proclamation functions as a tactic within a constellation of activities that groups might undertake to achieve those strategic goals. But what drives *this instance* of public proclamation? What do we hope will happen as a result of our speaking? Here we want to be intentional about how we hope people will respond to our public proclamation. If we consider the context of our speaking in terms of other speakers and the intentions of the gathering, as well as how it is connected to the strategic goals, we can name a specific purpose for our public proclamation that can point us toward the right content, shape, and tone (the focus of the following two chapters) as we begin to craft the speech.

Again, for those who preach, this is not an entirely foreign practice. Long calls this the "function statement," which is "a description of what the preacher hopes the sermon will create or cause to happen for the hearers. Sermons make demands on the hearers, which is another way of saying that they provoke change in the hearers (even if the change is a deepening of something already present). The function statement names the hoped-for change."[20] Similarly, Frank Thomas calls this the "behavioral purpose statement." This statement "forces the preacher to state specifically the way in which the sermon is to influence the behavior of the listener. No preacher can totally predict the behavioral result of any sermon, but

---

20. Long, *Witness of Preaching*, 127.

the Holy Spirit can encounter the listener in fresh and dynamic ways if the preacher prayerfully targets a behavioral result, and then carefully focuses the sermon toward that result."[21] A closer look at Thomas's method shows that his behavioral purpose statement combines what we have variously identified as a focus statement, sermon summary statement, central claim, and so on, with this statement about the sermon's purpose. Thomas has a fill-in-the-blank formula for what this statement should look like: "I propose _____ to the end hearers will _____."[22]

Some might worry that this intentionality around purpose is manipulative. Let me be clear: Our purpose should never be to manipulate or use authoritarian rhetorical devices so that people take the kind of action that we want. If, as I suggested in the first chapter, we imagine that public proclamation is part of an ongoing theological conversation, then the nature of that conversation is never manipulative. It does operate as a kind of leadership with purpose, but it does not foreclose possibilities to think, feel, or act otherwise.

To draw one more time from Schade, Sumney, and Askew, I appreciate the language they use in calling this statement the "central purpose." Similar to Thomas and Long, they define the central purpose as "stat[ing] in one sentence what the sermon aims to do and why."[23] For the authors, the central purpose is informed by both the central question and central claim, and they recommend the following format for constructing the central purpose statement: "The central purpose of this sermon is to [VERB] [OBJECT] so that [VERB] [OBJECT]." Or this option: "This sermon will [VERB] [OBJECT] in order to [VERB] [OBJECT]." Or, finally, this way: "This sermon [PRESENT TENSE VERB] [OBJECT] resulting in [NOUNS]."[24] Notice the connective language in these three possibilities: "so that," "in order to," and "resulting in." This kind of language indicates purpose. One example they use for a sermon is, "The central purpose of this sermon is to break open our limited conceptions of a 'male' God so that we may embrace the 'female' images of the Divine and expand the ways we encounter grace."[25] These options give us a sense that, for the authors, the sermon does not just *say* something, it also attempts to *do* something.

---

21. Frank A. Thomas, *They Like to Never Quit Praisin' God: The Role of Celebration in Preaching*, rev. and updated ed. (Pilgrim, 2013), 96.
22. Thomas, 96.
23. Schade, Sumney, and Askew, *Introduction to Preaching*, 173.
24. Schade, Sumney, and Askew, 175
25. Schade, Sumney, and Askew, 175.

We want to be equally intentional about articulating our purposes for public proclamation. We can use similar formulas to the authors' suggestions, focusing on what we hope will happen as a result of our public proclamation. Vital to these statements is the use of verbs that can ignite our sense of purpose. Some of these verbs might be connected to our central claim, which could draw from the four types of theological claims. In this case, we might say that a purpose of an instance of public proclamation could be to "offer judgment," "to provide reasons," "to explain/reframe/offer counterwitness," or "give permission," as long as we fill in the rest of the central purpose statement with a "so that," "in order to," or "resulting in." These are just beginning possibilities, using what we have already traced. Just as the authors invite us to focus on "vigorous verbs" for sermons,[26] so, too, should we focus on verbs that can play a pivotal role in articulating the purpose of our public proclamation. For instance, while this list is in no way exhaustive, I would offer the following list of beginning possibilities:

agitate	foster empathy
build coalitions	inspire
call to account	lament
celebrate	offer comfort
denounce	persuade
disturb	stand in solidarity
encourage	support
energize	unite
engage in critical thinking	witness to
express outrage	

These verbs help us get specific about a movement toward action of some sort. Since overwhelm, complacency, justice fatigue, impostor syndrome, and learned helplessness can keep us immobile, we need to consider what our speaking is inviting people into. Being as specific as possible about who the listeners are is important as well. Sermons are understandably directed toward congregations. This is not the case for public proclamation, so the more specific we can be, the better.

Continuing to build on the previous examples, I offer here some possible central purpose statements. First, I consider the imagined address to the city council after the murder of Sonya Massey. Our central claim was this: "Because God's love for all people makes a way

---

26. Schade, Sumney, and Askew, 175–76.

for peace, justice, and nonviolence, we condemn the police murder of Sonya Massey as an affront to God's ways in the world." Because we are addressing the city council in this scenario, we would want to not only offer our theological judgment but also move council members toward action that can prevent more instances of police violence. A possible central purpose statement might look like this: "The purpose of this public proclamation is to declare God's condemnation of violence in order to persuade the city council to take corrective action on policing." Notice how the central purpose statement names the city council. While others in the city council chambers will hear the speech, it is directed toward the city council. You might consider how a different audience or setting for this instance of public proclamation might change the purpose. In a community vigil, it might be more appropriate for the latter half of the central purpose statement to "express outrage," "lament," or invite some other appropriate action for the audience.

Second, we also consider Hord Owens's contribution to the Poor People's Campaign launch. The central claim was, "God's imperative that loving our neighbor is love of God requires us to collectively seek the good of those who are impoverished by political, economic, and social systems." I pointed out earlier that the press conference format implies a diffuse audience of listeners with different vantage points and affiliations. Since Hord Owens is but one of many speakers, I would suggest that she has a general audience in mind, especially those who at least have some openness to Christianity. I would also offer that clergy and laypeople associated with the Christian Church (Disciples of Christ) are especially part of her intended audience. As such, "This public proclamation reminds listeners of God's imperative to love our neighbors through collectively seeking the good of those who are impoverished, resulting in energizing all Christians, and members of the Christian Church (Disciples of Christ) in particular, to support the Poor People's Campaign." Notice the verbs "remind" and "energize." Loving God through love of neighbor is not a new concept, but it gives a familiar and theologically grounded warrant for a new action. The press conference format, with so many different voices from across many representative groups, is an opportune time to energize those who are listening to give their support.

Note that in both central purpose statements, I have also connected the purpose language to the strategic goal. The critical context remains important. While the strategic goal does not need to be in every central purpose statement as a rule, its presence in the statement helps us to be specific about what we intend with this instance of public proclamation.

Again, as with the central claim, you might try to formulate central purpose statements for the other two scenarios I have already described. When we practice these, we become more adept and proficient at doing this work more quickly when the need arises.

CONCLUSION

In this chapter, I have invited us to adapt some (perhaps) familiar preaching practices in order to facilitate our preparation for public proclamation. These three sentences—the theological claim, the central claim, and the central purpose—along with the critical context, help us to enter into the writing stage with a better sense of how our theological commitments inform what we will say, what it is we want to say, and what we hope will happen as a result. To put these concepts into practice, I invite you to engage in the following exercises before proceeding.

EXERCISE YOUR VOICE

—If you are experienced in public proclamation, read, watch, or listen to a previous instance of your public proclamation. Working backward, try to identify the theological claim, critical context, central claim, and central purpose in what you have said. Are you able to identify them with clarity? If not, how might one or more of the sentences have helped you?
  - Analyze the language you used in this instance. Where would you situate it along the continuum of faith-rooted language?

—If you are not experienced in public proclamation, continue to imagine the scenario you've been working on in previous chapters. Formulate the theological claim, critical context, central claim, and central purpose that would be fitting for your scenario. They might need some revision as you move forward and begin to write. That's okay. What matters is not that you have them precisely now, but that you will before you speak.
  - Think about the imagined setting and your own sense of identity. Considering the continuum of faith-rooted language described in the chapter, what do you think would be most appropriate for this instance of public proclamation?

5
The Shape of Public Proclamation
Form and Design

Having established the general direction of what we want to say through our theological and central claims and identifying the central purpose of our instance of proclamation, now is the time in our preparation for fleshing things out. Whether our public proclamation will be a three-minute speech before a city council, a five- to ten-minute speech at a public gathering to raise funds, or a longer address where we are perhaps the main speaker, we cannot ignore intentional arrangement of our thoughts as a way of moving our listeners toward the strategic goals we have identified. Thus, this chapter invites us to consider the question *What kind of rhetorical-communicative strategy will best help achieve the goal(s)?*

Here again, there are some crossovers from sermon preparation. Those who preach are accustomed to thinking about sermon forms (alternatively, design or structure—I use these terms interchangeably) and determining what particular form might best aid the sermon in accomplishing its goals. In other words, preachers are already familiar with the concept that the what and the how of a sermon are intricately related. The past generation of scholarship in preaching has firmly ensconced this in many of our preaching practices, confident that preachers should not simply shoehorn all sermons into a particular form. The idea here is that because what we are saying differs each week, as do our sermonic purposes, then we cannot use the same sermon forms week in and week out because form has a great deal to do with how we *experience* a sermon as listeners.

When I raise the idea of planning for the experience of listening, some of us may pause or even balk. We are rightly concerned about the kinds of authoritarian preaching and public speaking that can turn toward the manipulative by use of some of the devices we explore in this chapter. This concern is more than fair. However, consider for a moment one or more compelling yet firmly grounded sermons or instances of public proclamation. How did they make you feel? What was your experience as you listened to them? Now, do you think that the speaker attended to the experience of listening in their planning and in the moment of speaking? How so? There is truth to the often-cited proverb: "I've learned that people will forget what you said, people will forget what you did, but people will never forget how you made them feel."[1] But in our best instances of public speech, I believe the impact of the words we say and how we make people feel can work together and persist long after we have finished speaking.

We are right to be concerned about the possibilities for rhetorical transgression. Our global history and current events give us every right to raise our collective eyebrows with skepticism at the abuse of rhetoric. This is why I have structured the chapters of this book in the way that I have, encouraging each of us to think about the theological grounding of our public proclamation, our place and power, and the theological claims that we want to make in a particular instance of public proclamation. If we were to start with technique without accounting for the things that ground us toward an openhearted, gracious, and just theological orientation, then I would be more concerned about the potential dangers inherent to a rhetoric-first focus. Our deep theological reflection and careful discernment are important—nay, indispensable—steps along the way to having something to say in the public square.

In this chapter and in chapter 6, I want to focus on four specific areas that help us develop an appropriate rhetorical-communicative strategy for our instances of public proclamation. First, and as I have already mentioned, thinking about the form, design, or structure of our public proclamation helps us to develop a general design and arc of our speech. This chapter takes up that focus, considering design that can help structure the experience of listening in ways that are most appropriate to our central claims and central purposes. Second, we need a variety of appropriate devices for concretizing, supporting, and energizing the claims we make in our speaking. Third, we must think about the artistry of the language we use, as well as

---

1. Carl W. Buehner quoted in Richard L. Evans, *Richard Evans' Quote Book* (Publisher's, 1971), 244.

the related emotional tone of our speaking. Fourth and finally, but certainly not least, public proclamation involves more than carefully planned words. Our words are embodied in significant ways, and we do well to think about how our bodies can serve public proclamation in ways that support what we are saying. These concerns are the focus of chapter 6.

These final chapters are intertwined with one another. It is difficult to talk about form or design of public proclamation without also talking about concretizing devices, the artistry of language, emotion or tone, as well as embodiment. If you need to, feel free to read these chapters out of order. And if you are more familiar with rhetorical terms, these chapters discuss arrangement, style, and delivery.

FORM AND DESIGN

Just as form and design matter for sermons, so, too, does it matter for public proclamation. Form, design, and structure (terms I use interchangeably) link the what of our proclamation with the how for public proclamation. Thinking deliberatively about form aids listeners with a pattern for remembering what has been said. It also provides listeners with a framework or an arc to follow, both in terms of the sequence of the message and its emotional flow. Attention to form, as suggested earlier, considers the experience of listening—or to choose a more active term, the experience of *participation* in public proclamation. Below, I detail sermon forms that can help structure public proclamation: one form from community organizing literature and a sampling of forms that come from the discipline of public speaking. These are most certainly not exhaustive, and as you read through them, you might think about ways that there could be creative exchange among them or forms that emerge more naturally from central claim statements.

Helpful Forms from Homiletics

Eugene Lowry and the Lowry Loop

Eugene Lowry's classic text *The Homiletical Plot* sets forth a narrative, plot-shaped sermon form. According to Lowry, "One might say that any sermon involves both an 'itch' and a 'scratch' and sermons are born when at least implicitly in the preacher's mind the problematic *itch* intersects with a solutional *scratch*—between the particularity of the human predicament and the particularity of the gospel."[2] Before moving into the finer details of Lowry's design, popularly known as "the Lowry Loop," it is worth noting that the work we have already done in preparation provides a pathway here. Because we will have identified the central claim and named the critical context where a problem is occurring, we will well know both the itch (or problem, via the critical context) and the scratch through our theological and central claims and awareness of strategic goals.

Lowry plots a sermon along the lines of a narrative plot, and the different pieces of the sermon work together seamlessly in sequence and ultimately constitute an "event-in-time . . . a process and not a collection of parts," as with other kinds of deductive sermon forms that have parts that operate independently and could be easily rearranged without much impact on the listening experience. For Lowry, this movement of the sermon is arranged in a way that proceeds from problem to solution or ambiguity to clarity through a series of stages that he identifies as such: (1) upsetting the equilibrium, (2) analyzing the discrepancy, (3) disclosing the clue to resolution, (4) experiencing the gospel, and (5) anticipating the consequences. In shorthand, Lowry identifies these stages as (1) Oops, (2) Ugh, (3) Aha, (4) Whee, and (5) Yeah.[3] For sermons, stage 3 is almost always generated from interaction with the biblical text and the resulting theological claim.

To put Lowry's design into more practical terms and adapt it for public proclamation, we would keep the general design the same. Allow me to offer the following possibility: In the contentious and divided atmosphere of the 2024 election cycle, a clergy colleague gathered with clergy from multiple faith traditions outside their city hall to promote civic unity and to encourage fellow citizens to act with kindness toward neighbors with differing political stances.[4] In such a setting, a speaker could operate with the Lowry Loop this way:

---

2. Eugene L. Lowry, *The Homiletical Plot: The Sermon as Narrative Art Form*, exp. ed. (Westminster John Knox, 2000), 19.

3. Lowry, 26.

4. This action might seem disconnected from policy or strategic efforts toward justice. It could even be viewed as performative or dismissive of significant justice concerns in a community or across the nation. My thanks to Kristin Peters for raising this concern. Throughout this book, I want to suggest a range of possible scenarios in which faith leaders might be engaged. This could very well serve as a starting point for building interfaith collaboration and more strategic justice work in a community or as an entry point for others who had not previously been involved if the work of this group had started prior to this moment. I recognize that I have not provided a deep dive on the context for the action or detailed its outcomes.

1. Identifying the problem of our division in the current US political atmosphere.
2. Citing stories and examples that not only clarify the problem but also explore its effects as well. Here, the speaker might talk about how children are affected or name particular instances of deepening conflict in the community. In a mode of critical thought, the speaker might explore who benefits by our division and enmity toward one another.
3. Uncovering the principle of kindness, filtered through a faith-rooted perspective in a way that matches how the faith leader wants to show up, remembering that this is a continuum. For instance, the leader could cite from Galatians 5:22 and part of the fruit of the Spirit being kindness as a natural outgrowth of faith in the Christian tradition. Illustrative connections between fruit and agriculture would be available here, especially in the summertime when this took place.
4. Expressing what happens or what could happen when kindness is extended between neighbors. Here specific and concrete instances would help people imagine what the community could be like.
5. Ending with exhortations to live with kindness in such ways that help realize the type of community that people idealize and for which they say that they strive.

Lowry provides us with a design in which it is possible to allow people to name whatever problem is being addressed as a problem and to collectively experience the effects and examine them with a critical eye. Not content to leave it there, a speaker can uncover a faith-rooted resolution and imagine a world in which that resolution is set in motion, providing call and motivation to work toward a strategic goal, individually and collectively.

Frank Thomas and Celebrative Design

Frank Thomas's sermonic design in *They Like to Never Quit Praisin' God* shares similarities with Lowry, but with some distinct differences.[5] Whereas Lowry's plot moves through five stages, Thomas's "celebrative design" has three: (1) situation/complication, (2) gospel assurance to complication, and (3) resolution celebration. We can easily see the similarities in the stages

---

5. Frank A. Thomas, *They Like to Never Quit Praisin' God: The Role of Celebration in Preaching*, rev. ed. (Pilgrim, 2013).

just from the titles. Thomas brings at least two important differences to his design. First, whereas Lowry focuses on narrative plots that are guided solely by cognitive logic, Thomas incorporates a more holistic representation of human thought and behavioral processes through emphasizing the role of what he calls "emotive logic." Incorporating the thought of Edwin Friedman, Thomas proposes that the use of language around emotion

> does not mean paying attention to feelings typically known as emotions but to the emotional context in which communication takes place. . . . It is precisely because so much of Western preaching has ignored emotional context and process, and focused on cerebral process and words, that homileticians most recently have struggled for new methods to effectively communicate the gospel.[6]

Here, Thomas calls attention to the genius of preaching in African American traditions and redirects homiletics at large to the importance of emotion as a mode of appeal in sermons that can shift both belief and action. Second, and related to the preceding sentence, Thomas lifts up the practice and sermonic moment of celebration, characteristic of much of the preaching in African American sermonic traditions. For Thomas, celebration is not just an unreflective cookie-cutter sermonic moment or style of closing the sermon but characteristic of what he calls

> celebrative design [that] intends, as part of the emotional process of the sermon, emotive movement similar to musical movement. The sermon is a series of ideas and images (moves) expressed in bundles of language that generate a certain nuance or shade of meaning that registers in the emotive. Each move builds upon the emotive effect of the previous move, heightening and enhancing what has already been created, until at the close of the sermon, one is left with a clear meaning or experience that registers in the intuitive. The sermon does not ignore the cognitive to secure the emotive movement, but includes it as part of the process. . . . Celebrative design does not intend to move people for the sake of moving people [emotionally]; rather it intends to move people as part of the process of impacting core belief.[7]

Thomas understands the significant role that the emotive plays in transforming belief and behavior and highlights that inherent understanding in African American preaching traditions. I take time to name the importance

---

6. Thomas, 19–20.
7. Thomas, 26.

of emotion because of natural fears surrounding emotional manipulation in speech, both in church and in the public square. However, as Thomas recognizes, "The most effective preachers understand that cognitive logic and emotive logic are not separated in the sermon but are partners that take or yield priority at the appropriate stage of the sermon to facilitate the upward movement to celebration in intuitive core belief."[8]

Since Thomas's first two moves are so similar to Lowry's first three, I do not trace them here, except to say that Thomas integrates emotional connection through these first two moves of the sermon, especially in the opening move of situation-complication, planning for emotive logic that can help people identify a shared concern. In terms of the final move of the sermon, Thomas defines celebration as "the joyful and ecstatic reinforcement of the truth already taught in the main body of the sermon."[9] Thomas goes on to name the materials of celebration this way: "affirmative and joyous emotion with the beauty and flow of poetry, music, and art are the rule and standard. Poetry, heightened rhetoric, creative imagery, hyperbole, and embellished language are all suitable vehicles for expression of the profoundly joyous and hopeful disposition of celebration."[10]

What might this look like for public proclamation? To return to the example of clergy and other community leaders advocating kindness outside city hall, celebration might draw from the cognitive logic (theological claim) that all humans are made in the image of God, and thus we are freed from what might be burdensome or dispassionate civic obligations or reciprocal expectations to treat others with kindness. Instead, when we recognize the Divine in each other, we are freed to act accordingly, resulting in a kind of liberated practice of kindness. In order to tap into the emotive logic and experiential connection, the speaker might tell stories or give examples of this kind of kindness; find poetry, music, or art that helps us experience or reinforces this kind of kindness; or otherwise engage the kind of heightened, poetic, and joyous language that helps listeners feel the freedom of kindness rooted in recognition of the Divine in others.[11] Thus, a critical question to ask for planning this move of public proclamation would be, What does it *feel like* to experience, participate in, offer, or receive the resolution of the theological claim connected with the strategic

---

8. Thomas, 113.
9. Thomas, 108
10. Thomas, 123.
11. Note that while I am lifting up Thomas's example of celebration that is rooted in African American traditions of preaching, I am not advocating for those who identify as white to engage in mimicry or appropriation in ways that are outside their voice and identity.

goal? While it might not be appropriate for every occasion of public proclamation, Thomas's celebrative design does make a path for the kind of public proclamation that seeks to uplift even as it seeks to shift belief and practice.

As I mentioned, there are nearly endless forms of sermon design that might be transferable into the realm of public proclamation. In each consideration, I would encourage speakers to be guided by theological claims, central claims, and central purposes that include strategic goals so that each instance of public proclamation operates by the good homiletical wisdom that integrates the what of speaking with the how.

Forms That Honestly Respond to Trauma

The forms just outlined are built on the kind of logics that supply resolution, the easing of tension, or a clear path forward. However, recent work in homiletics asks us to be more honest in our preaching and about the preaching context. Sometimes we cannot provide easy answers, and sometimes there are no strategic goals other than to provide space for lament and establish human connections. In instances of human-made or natural disaster, to enter into public proclamation that rushes toward theological answers or hastily made strategic goals can skip past the horror, trauma, and fragmentation that people might experience. According to Chuck Campbell,

> Too many preachers, myself included, likewise rush too quickly to escape the interval of the grotesque. That's our purpose, isn't it? Surely our goal is clarity, security, certainty. Give people a nice, focused nugget to carry home—not the shocking, unresolved contradictions of a grotesque gospel. . . . For when we rush to order, when we avoid the interval of the grotesque, our preaching may become shallow, unreal, clichéd. And we end up falsifying both the gospel and life itself—we end up imposing false patterns. The grotesque gospel, however, calls preachers to relinquish our familiar patterns.[12]

Relinquishing our familiar, narrative- or problem-solution-based patterns that resolve tension can be especially helpful when public proclamation is faced with situations of trauma and unfathomable evil.

Kimberly Wagner describes responses to experiences of trauma as "narrative fracture," that is, when we are not able to (re)establish a coherent narrative of our lives in response to traumatic events. In response,

---

12. Charles L. Campbell, *The Scandal of the Gospel: Preaching and the Grotesque* (Westminster John Knox, 2021), 11–12.

she advocates for preaching that "acknowledges the incomplete and broken nature of trauma, suffering, and narrative fracture by refusing to fill in the blanks or manufacture clear connections between the fragments of experience."[13] One such form that she advocates is the "Frayed-Edges Form."[14] By this, Wagner suggests that

> sermons constructed in the Frayed-Edges Form may still employ some narrative arcs, connections between moves, or themes and ideas that move the sermon along. But the signature feature of this form is the way it resists coherence by rejecting any kind of tidy resolution or redemptive ending. Put another way, the Frayed-Edges Form demonstrates an unwillingness to sacrifice truth for coherence.[15]

In translating this approach to public proclamation, we might follow some familiar patterns. What we should not do is wrap things up at the end, providing resolution, conclusion, or challenge. Instead, we might end with stories that leave us in liminal space or with questions or suggestions that allow participants to live into the inconsistencies and tensions they are experiencing. This kind of permission-giving can be a humanizing honesty in moments of shock, grief, and trauma.

As Wagner notes about preaching, leaving public proclamation unfinished can feel as if we have not done what many of us have been trained to do—that is, leave people with hope, resolution, or a clear call to action. However, she goes on to say, "a narratively fractured congregation [or public] is affirmed for where they are and promised . . . that 'God is in the boat' with them."[16] In other words, the theological affirmation here is that God is present through suffering and doubt, even when life does not make sense. This can be a helpful theological reframing (see chapter 4) for public witness.

A Design from Community Organizing

Marshall Ganz and Public Narrative

Marshall Ganz is an experienced community organizer and currently serves as a lecturer in the Harvard Kennedy School, with research

---

13. Kimberly R. Wagner, *Fractured Ground: Preaching in the Wake of Mass Trauma* (Westminster John Knox, 2023), 82.
14. Wagner, 91.
15. Wagner, 91.
16. Wagner, 103.

focusing on leadership, organizing, and action. In his book *People, Power, Change: Organizing for Democratic Renewal*, Ganz focuses on the power of storytelling and "public narrative" to help organizers think through compelling modes of communication in their work.[17] According to Ganz, public narrative is "a way we can harness the power of narrative to the work of leadership: accepting responsibility for enabling others to achieve shared purpose under conditions of uncertainty."[18] Such uses of narrative can "construct an empathetic bridge with others to enable them to respond mindfully to the disruptive impact of loss, difference, domination, and change."[19] As such, Ganz encourages speakers to weave narratives that can unite those who will hear as a way of encouraging new, shared identities that can propel initiatives and movements forward into their work.

Before discussing the form that Ganz proposes, we should acknowledge preaching's long history with narrative. As a result of the New Homiletic that emerged in the late 1960s, many preachers moved solidly into hermeneutical and homiletical approaches that foregrounded narrative. From Fred Craddock's inductive movement to Eugene Lowry's aforementioned "homiletical plot" to David Buttrick's sense of plots in sermon structure, it is safe to say that a generation (or two or three) has deep formation in how narrative operates in sermons.[20] What's more, recent reactions have sought to pull the pendulum back in terms of a full-throated confidence in the power of narrative, namely in Thomas Long's reassessment of narrative preaching and Charles Campbell's approach to narrative and the grotesque in everyday life.[21] Suffice it to say, most preachers have already encountered some of the ink spilled in thinking about how narrative impacts preaching. People with some experience in narrative preaching may recognize a connection in what will follow from Ganz with what Thomas Troeger and Nora Tisdale call the "My Story, Biblical Story, Our (Congregational) Story" design that they identify in a sermon from Edmund Steimle.[22]

---

17. Marshall Ganz, *People, Power, Change: Organizing for Democratic Renewal* (Oxford University Press, 2024), 56–88.
18. Ganz, 58.
19. Ganz, 58–59.
20. For a quick orientation, see John S. McClure, *Preaching Words: 144 Key Terms in Homiletics* (Westminster John Knox, 2007), 90–94.
21. See Thomas G. Long, *Preaching from Memory to Hope* (Westminster John Knox, 2009); Campbell, *Scandal of the Gospel*.
22. Leonora Tubbs Tisdale and Thomas H. Troeger, *A Sermon Workbook: Exercises in the Art and Craft of Preaching* (Abingdon, 2013), 76.

Ganz has confidence in using narratives in public speaking for change, insofar as it can articulate a shared experience and invite people into collective action. To do that, Ganz proposes a tripartite structure for public speaking, inspired by the first-century BCE Jewish leader Rabbi Hillel. Ganz describes it this way:

> I tell a story of *self* to evoke experience of values that called me to accept leadership. I tell a story of *us* to evoke shared values that can enable agency in choosing a response. I tell a story of *now* to evoke experience of the urgent challenge to those values that demands a response now, the sources of hope to enable the agency to choose well, and clarity as to the choices we must make to respond.[23]

In shorthand, we can call this form "Story of Self, Story of Us, Story of Now."

The first section encourages speakers to share from their own journeys, life experiences, and actions, particularly moments when a situation demanded a response, when they made choices, experienced some sort of outcome (good, bad, or neutral), or learned something significant. The desire here is to communicate something of the values from which the speaker operates, as well as the meaning they are constructing out of their story, and why they have chosen a particular course of action.[24] Ganz encourages speakers in this section to know how they experience "the world's hurt" and "the world's hope" as a way of fostering authenticity.

The second section operates out of the recognition that "for a collection of people to become an 'us' requires an interpreter of shared experience, a storyteller. In a social movement, the interpretation of the movement's new experience is a critical leadership function."[25] The process of finding and shaping stories of us requires discernment in thinking through how the stories move us toward shared values, whether that is thinking about knitting different communities together or encouraging listeners to separate themselves from their current communities. The story of us is the work of inviting people into solidarity based on shared values for the common cause, even if their experiences differ.

The third and final movement uses narrative to frame "a challenge we face, a choice we can make, and an outcome that may result. In fact, a story of now is when story and strategy come together—when

---

23. Ganz, *People, Power, Change*, 70.
24. Ganz, 70.
25. Ganz, 73.

the why we need to do what we need to do (story) joins the how we could do what we need to do (strategy)."[26] Here Ganz also emphasizes the need to communicate urgency—whether that is through expressing the challenges and threats to shared values, highlighting urgent needs, or naming present opportunities—all while being very specific about what we are asking of people.[27] This sense of urgency and specificity of what we are asking of people is deeply connected to what we have covered earlier in terms of central purpose and strategic goals. Stories that cannot point to or invite people into concrete, specific actions will fail to mobilize people.

Ganz notes the importance of linking these three narratives together as a form of public leadership. The practice of weaving them together helps speakers do the work I have named earlier in connecting speaking to strategic goals and also forms coherence within public proclamation. In addition, Ganz suggests that the order of these three stories can be shuffled, as long as the resulting public narrative is coherent, makes sense, flows in a way that can be followed, and opens up an invitation to act in some way.

Additional Designs from Public Speaking

Finally, I want to explore a few organizational designs from the discipline of public speaking and communication that provide additional templates to help us think about the experience of listening. Again, I would caution us not to use these as templates into which we shoehorn public proclamation without thinking about our communicative purpose, lest we choose a design that fails to account for what we want our public proclamation to do and how we want listeners to experience it. Not to be reductive, but basic literature on public speaking outlines four different basic types of speeches: information, instruction, entertainment, and persuasion. A more nuanced understanding detects hybrid forms of these types. For instance, comedy is a type of speech that is primarily identified as entertainment but can also be marked by the purposes of persuasion and information. Many of us have experienced comedy that was intended not just to make us laugh but also to change our perspectives and move us toward different positions and actions.[28] The types of speeches that we would naturally

---

26. Ganz, 75.
27. Ganz, 75.
28. For more on this in relation to preaching, see Jacob D. Myers, *Stand-Up Preaching: Homiletical Insights from Contemporary Comedians* (Cascade Books, 2022).

be inclined to borrow from this literature would be under the category of persuasive. I want to hold open the possibility for hybrid forms. Thus, in forms that might be designated as informative, I suggest here that we could adjust or add components to the speech form that would help us in our persuasive purposes.

Problem-Solution Pattern

The problem-solution pattern helps frame problems and solutions to help alleviate the problems.[29] In keeping with the earlier scenario on kindness, this kind of public proclamation might move from naming the overall problem of division in our political climate to the solution of kindness. In the first part of the public proclamation, the speaker would detail why the problem functions as a problem and then, in the second part, how the solution works toward relief. Quite basic in terms of its format, the pattern could aid listeners by engaging in critical thinking about the problem and solutions, which is particularly useful in a climate where people tend to deal in broad-based generalities and characterizations rather than grappling with the specific reasons and implications of problems and solutions.

Cause-Effect / Effect-Cause

This pattern seeks to draw connections between cause(s) and effect(s) between two or more elements.[30] The pattern here has a similar bipartite design, although here the major elements are reversible. If we were to plot our kindness example on the effect-cause pattern, we might begin by describing the ways that civic division and strife are on the increase, noting the specific ways that these effects are manifesting in a community. The second half of the public proclamation would describe the factors or causes of why this situation has evolved. A missing element here is a division for offering solutions, which is where we would want to modify the design with a kind of "hinge" or "aha" (Lowry) rooted in our central claim that helps us toward strategic goals. For example, a simple connection might go something like this: "But friends, we cannot go on living like this! There is too much at stake and too much to lose in us allowing our political differences to separate us. At the core

---

29. Joseph A. DeVito, *Human Communication: The Basic Course*, 10th ed. (Allyn and Bacon, 2005), 314.
30. DeVito, 314.

of my faith tradition is the recognition that each of us is made in God's image. And that commitment encourages me to recognize you not for your political commitments but to ground my relationship to you with a recognition of your inherent worth and dignity as God's creation." From there, we could easily move toward language that leads us toward shared recognition of one another's worth and dignity.

Motivated Sequence

The motivated sequence pattern suggests the following five divisions: attention, need, satisfaction, visualization, and action. The first step is the most obvious: using some device to gain the listener's attention before moving into a section that establishes that a need among the listeners must be met. The third section offers that which will fill the need among the listeners, and the fourth invites them to use their imaginations to envision "the situation as it would be if the need were satisfied as you suggested"[31] in the previous section. Finally, the speaker moves to advising the listeners of what action they should take in order to realize that which has been experienced as a need and imagined as being fulfilled.

With public proclamation in mind, there are resonances with both Lowry and Thomas. There is also a sense that the work of visualization in the fourth section could be wholly based on the kind of theological imagination that works to cast the world as being fulfilled by God's purposes.[32] To take up our kindness example again, we might imagine moving from descriptions of our need for neighborliness to satisfaction through imagining what the community would be like if we all took the mindset offered. Inviting listeners to imagine in that language or by other means can be a powerful device. For instance, this is exactly what King does in the latter parts of his "I Have a Dream" speech. The repetition of "I have a dream" and its constituent parts invites listeners to imagine the satisfaction of the need for freedom and equality that are at the heart of King's civic and theological imagination.

Structure-Function

While textbooks offer the structure-function pattern as an informative speech pattern, in the hands of those engaged in public proclamation,

---

31. DeVito, 316.

32. See, for instance, the way I discuss the "radical imagination" in Richard William Voelz, *Preaching to Teach: Inspire People to Think and Act* (Abingdon, 2019), 35–50.

we can see something quite different. The structure-function pattern "is well suited to discuss how something is constructed (its structural aspects) and what it does (its functional aspects)."[33] In the case of our kindness example, these preliminary informative components would seek to highlight the realities of our civic division, its structural features, and its structural beginnings (by social media, news media, and our narrow individual, familial, or economic interests), followed by descriptions of how that structural division functions. For instance, our divisions often financially benefit those who seek to perpetuate mistrust, further exacerbate marginalization, disadvantage the vulnerable, and stall political goodwill and activity, just to name a few. Moving beyond analysis and information would be critical to completing the public proclamation, with a rejection of not only the structure but its functions as well, in favor of new or renewed structures that can serve the collective good. It would be important to highlight how kindness can infuse the new structures we imagine together, especially from faith-rooted perspectives.

Comparison and Contrast

A comparison-and-contrast pattern might initially be considered a useful informative speech pattern, but it can also be cast as a mode for public proclamation when comparing and contrasting two or more modes of being and response. In connection with the structure-function pattern and with the kindness example, comparison and contrast might pit civic division fueled by political, corporate, and individual interests against a vision of civic life inspired by a vision of life in community that lies at the heart of the Christian faith tradition. This example of the comparison-and-contrast pattern could function as a strict appeal to those listeners who identify as Christian or cast in such a way that it has a broad appeal to people with different or no faith backgrounds.

As with the examples from homiletical literature, these patterns from public speaking are not exhaustive. And as I have tried to show, creative combinations can help structure public proclamation in ways that move beyond informative purposes toward more persuasive ones, as well as beyond simple logical appeals toward appeals rooted in our hard-won theological claims and central claims.

33. DeVito, *Human Communication*, 317.

CONCLUSION

Those of us involved in public proclamation should take great care in how we design our instances of speaking. As noted at the chapter's outset, design/form accounts not just for the content and words but also for the experience of listening in how public proclamation exhibits unity and coherence and how it makes others feel. These designs help us construct the larger moves of an instance of public proclamation. While some speakers consider this process as a kind of outline, I encourage them to think of the individual blocks of a storyboard in order to visualize the ways that these large moves or units of thought function. A storyboard helps us consider the energy and flow of an instance of public proclamation, but thinking in this way can also help us with recall and memory in efforts to speak without complete manuscripts. With some larger designs in mind, in the next chapter I encourage us to consider how we fill in these larger units of thought with devices that touch the life experiences of those who gather to listen and participate, with language that dances and that involves our bodies.

EXERCISE YOUR VOICE

- —As we have done before, if you are more experienced with public proclamation, find a speech and analyze its form, design, or structure. What are the major building blocks of this instance of public proclamation? How do they relate to each other? Can you identify one of the patterns described in this chapter? Or does something new emerge?
- —If you are less experienced, continue to consider the instance of public proclamation you have been imagining. What form, design, or structure might work best? What changes if you were to use another design?

6
Dynamic Public Proclamation
Concretizing Devices, Lively Language, and Embodiment

The previous chapter focused on the organization of public proclamation—the structuring of larger units of thought to make our messaging clear, coherent, and purposeful. This chapter continues to answer the question raised before: *"What kind of rhetorical-communicative strategy will best help achieve the goal(s)?"* Here, however, we press beyond the larger units of thought and into the kinds of devices that render public proclamation concrete, the ways that we can plan for lively language, and, last but certainly not least, how we can think about our bodies as sites of expressive meaning-making that work synergistically for compelling and effective public proclamation.

While other chapters have included exercises at the end, in this chapter I have tried to embed them throughout, so as you read, pause to try out what I suggest. In addition, if you have been analyzing a previous instance of public proclamation, you might do the same as you read this chapter. If you have been working step-by-step as you have been reading to create an example of public proclamation, you can continue that work as you make your way through the chapter.

CONCRETIZING DEVICES

When I was in seminary and serving a congregation, my spouse and I rode home after worship one Sunday. I asked how she felt about the sermon I had just preached. While she was gracious to me as always, her feedback amounted to this: "The sermon was too abstract." Preachers and listeners know well that sermons fall flat if we fail to be concrete and connect to people's everyday lives. Ever since Jesus talked about mustard seeds and fig trees—and prophets before him used other vibrant images and symbols—preachers have sought illustrative material that sheds light on the ideas that we are trying to communicate. In the period called the New Homiletic, fresh insights into story and narrative led homileticians and preachers to think about how narrative, stories, and other ways of being concrete are not just ways to support our claims but they can function as the claim themselves. To use an oft-quoted maxim from Fred Craddock, the stories "are the point."[1]

John McClure helpfully shows how the "cultural code" within sermons functions as a significant "track" (an image borrowed from music recording) for those types of sermons that are mixed with theology, Bible, and message coding.[2] He demonstrates the different ways that our approach to culture can make a difference for the sermon's meaning. McClure's insights are important, especially insofar as they suggest that we pay deep attention to how our efforts to concretize make an impact on how sermons shape listeners' theological worldviews. I do not have the space here to unpack the specific ways McClure unfolds this, but I do want to echo his claim that the ways we concretize in our sermons, and therefore in public proclamation, matter deeply for theological and ethical formation over time.

Turning more specifically to public proclamation, we lose connection to people's real lives if we simply name the details or statistical efficacy of policies, share reams of data to support our position, advise people they should take certain actions, or do something else entirely. Doing so leaves listeners without connections to their own lives or their neighbors' lives, without emotional investment, without understanding the human element, and without insights that make real the issues we seek to address. Not being careful about the ways we concretize can run the danger of excluding, lifting up one group at the expense of another, demonizing, or placing limitations on who can understand what we might be saying. As McClure observes with regard to preaching,

---

1. Fred B. Craddock, *Preaching* (Abingdon, 2010), 204.
2. For an in-depth examination, see John S. McClure, *The Four Codes of Preaching: Rhetorical Strategies* (Westminster John Knox, 2004).

Sermon illustrations don't simply legitimate our message for the day. They also legitimate the culture to which they refer. If we turn "the illustration" over and look at its underside, we begin to see that illustrations are part of a larger, often unconscious cultural strategy in preaching in which they serve the purpose of both generating and legitimating an entire message-system or *culture* within the community of sermon-hearers.[3]

Put in simpler terms, when we seek to concretize in public proclamation, we should be careful about the cultural assumptions and values inherent to our concretizing devices. Do they represent only one, limited cultural view at the expense of others? Or can a wide variety of listeners access these devices, remembering that in public proclamation we are seeking to build solidarity and communal power amid differences? To help flesh this out, we turn now to some possibilities for concretizing our public proclamation.

Wisdom from Community Organizing: Issue Framing and Stories

From the field of community organizing, two important and interconnected strategies are helpful when planning for public proclamation. The first is the strategy of "issue framing," which Loretta Pyles defines as "intentional messaging crafted by changemakers to meaningfully communicate social justice issues to their audiences."[4] This is somewhat abstract, but Pyles suggests here that people walk around with assumptions, values, narratives, and understandings of the reasons an issue exists (causes), its impacts (effects), and the people who control and are affected by them. These "deep frames" are entrenched, settled understandings and approaches, formed culturally through our families of origin, educational experiences, social groups, media, and other factors.[5] Part of the work of communication in community organizing is to disrupt those deep frames and to replace them with new, truer, and more compelling frames that orient listeners toward collective work for justice. The idea is to take abstract concepts—we could pick any: from climate crisis, to domestic violence, to voting rights, to housing justice—and offer messaging that

---

3. John S. McClure, "The Other Side of Sermon Illustration," *Journal for Preachers* 12, no. 2 (1989): 2.
4. Loretta Pyles, *Progressive Community Organizing: Transformative Practice in a Globalizing World* (Taylor and Francis, 2021), 192.
5. Pyles, 192.

breaks through old frames of understanding and the status quo with new ways of understanding "that identify injustices, attribute blame, suggest solutions, and inspire collective action."[6]

Issue framing suggests that as those engaged in public proclamation, we engage in a few analytical questions:

1. *Status quo*: What is the status quo understanding of why a phenomenon or social problem exists?
2. *Opposition*: What is the opposition's understanding and communication around the phenomenon or social problem?
3. *Power*: Who bears responsibility? Who is affected? What processes keep the issue stuck or make it worse?
4. *Narratives*: What stories are often told that reflect these deep frames?
5. *Language*: What kinds of language are used that keeps the issue entrenched? Are there specific words or phrases that are reflected in the "deep frames"?

On the other side of these questions comes the work of offering new frames that shift the energy and galvanize collective power for change.

One of the most significant ways to offer a new frame is through stories. We have already seen that a story can be a powerful organizing device for public proclamation. At a closer level, stories can help us concretize issues and offer new frames for understanding and collective action. We can use stories to understand the deep frames, or what we might call "stories of harm," and we can develop new stories for new frames, or what we might call "stories of hope." When doing so, Pyles suggests organizers consider the following elements of stories:

1. *Conflict*: Helping establish the point of view that is represented.
2. *Characters*: Understanding the key actors in the story.
3. *Imagery*: Identifying metaphors and evocative language to help the audience grasp the story easily.
4. *Foreshadowing*: Anticipating what is to come in the story (if we maintain the status quo or if we adopt a new frame and collective action).
5. *Underlying assumptions*: Identifying the unstated ideas and values that must be accepted for the story's validity.

---

6. Pyles, 193.

Story crafting and storytelling are significant acts for collective organizing and for individuals who are preparing for public proclamation. According to Pyles,

> This is where people get to use their creative capacities to envision another truth and to dream their world into reality. The story should challenge the underlying assumptions of the opposition's story, avoid reinforcing their assumptions, and uplift the assumptions and values of their group. Engaging imagery and characters are used to clarify the conflict and move the audience to a clear choice. The story offers clarity on what the consequences or cost could be for not embracing the right side of the conflict at the same time that it uplifts their own assumptions and opens up pathways to the desired outcomes.[7]

If you are working on a specific problem or issue now, this is a good place to pause and consider the stories of the deep frame and the story you want to tell to offer listeners perspective. Examine each of the elements listed here as you craft elements of the new story. What is the new story of the future you envision? Or if you have engaged in public proclamation before, select an instance and examine it using these categories as a kind of rubric. Did you include these elements? Was something left out? The capacity to craft these stories can be crucial for effectively and concretely communicating with listeners. You might also connect the practices of issue framing and stories to the forms explored in chapter 5.

Other Concretizing Devices

Stories are significant because they deal in the concrete, create points of identification, and evoke emotional responses. But they are not the only concretizing devices we have at our disposal. Every year in Richmond, Virginia, the faith-based community organizing group RISC (Richmonders Involved in Strengthening our Communities) gathers together for a collective action built around the issues the group has focused on in the previous year and will focus on in the year to come. At the 2023 meeting, I observed not only stories of harm and hope but a host of other concretizing devices that are worthy of our use, when they are appropriate.

---

7. Pyles, 197.

Identifying the Opposition

I have already highlighted that characters are part of building and telling the story, but I should mention again that clearly identifying and naming the opposition (*not* the enemy) to the strategic goal is important. Is the opposition what community organizers call the "target," the actual decision-maker?[8] Or is it a person (a government official), group (a cohort of government officials affiliated with a certain stance), entity (a corporation), or shared idea or policy (individualism) that functions as the opponent? Finding ways to name the opposition clearly and locating them in the system can be immensely helpful. Similarly, doing our homework to know the language the opposition uses can be helpful in a variety of ways, such as identifying misleading or false claims or appropriating the language in a way that lampoons the opposition's position or policy.

Naming Alliances and Emphasizing the Collective

On the other side of the opposition is naming alliances and emphasizing the collective. One of the biggest barriers to social change can be individuals thinking or feeling that problems are too big to tackle by themselves, even if these individuals are part of a smaller interest-based group. Naming how individuals are or could be coming together and cooperating beyond the individual or small-group level—and beyond some measure of identity-based or ideological differences—can be an empowering way of building collective power. Here I want to highlight the importance of naming intercultural alliances of all sorts. Finding ways to bring this out in the group, gathering, or action—if one is happening—can build solidarity among those participating and broaden the coalition. Being able to identify and talk about the "we," in examples of work done and strategic goals ahead, can give tangible ways of realizing that the burden for change is not just on individuals, if everyone shares in the work.

Emphasizing Ecumenical and Interfaith Solidarity/Sharing

Related to the previous device, especially for the work of faith-rooted public proclamation, is emphasizing ecumenical Christian and interfaith solidarity. When we can emphasize that whatever strategic goal we are

---

8. Pyles, 197.

working to achieve is something that multiple Christian perspectives and faith traditions share, the idea of community solidarity can galvanize and unify across difference. The Poor People's Campaign is exceptional at emphasizing such solidarity in its public messaging as a "moral movement" that is inclusive of multiple faith traditions and those who claim no religious faith at all.

Describing Vivid Details

This point may seem too obvious to mention, but we can easily get stuck at the level of policy or program, without emphasizing the details of what happens when the deep frames are allowed to continue or the possibilities of what could happen with new frames. For instance, RISC worked to win a substantial amount of money for a mobile home repair-and-replace program. When RISC held its yearly gathering, just the verbal descriptions of the condition of some of the mobile homes had a significant evocative effect on making the problem tangible, as well as lifting up the victories achieved when those homes were repaired or replaced.

Connecting with Visual Images

We undeniably live in a culture of images, and images that often compete for attention. By connecting our words to images, we can further concretize our messaging by providing examples. In addition to the vivid verbal descriptions of the mobile homes, key images were shown at the RISC gathering that helped people realize the poor conditions in which people were living, and the effects of RISC's achievement of a strategic goal in the after pictures of some of the mobile homes. This kind of visual concretizing can be an effective complement to speech. Consider if projection screens will be available in a gathering or if you can easily direct people to images on the internet they can see on their smartphones.

Incorporating Statistics and Data

Statistics and data are double-edged swords. Of course, they can be used in such a way that they overwhelm or bore with too much information, obfuscate salient features of a problem or solution, or sidestep real people affected by the issue under consideration. Care is needed when it comes to statistics and data. To be effective, we want to use data in an evocative way, bringing into stark realization a problem, identifying a specific need or request, or celebrating a strategic goal achieved. Find ways to connect data and statistics to stories, feelings, images, important ideas, and slogans.

Providing Definitions

When groups are gathered, especially across differences, it's good practice to not assume that everyone understands the terms we use. If some terms are especially new, niche, or specific to the gathering, take a moment to define those terms, which can draw people from feeling like an outsider to an insider and, as a result, foster intergroup understanding, support, and action. For instance, in RISC's work, "Affordable Housing Trust Fund" is a significant policy term that, left undefined, can cause confusion or an inability for individuals to connect to policy and advocacy efforts.

Using Analogies, Metaphors, and Similes

Last, but certainly not least, analogies, metaphors, and similes can be effective ways of helping us be more concrete through making comparisons.[9] In one RISC gathering, a speaker drew on a scene in an animated film in order to liken the group's collective work to that of forming a supportive human bridge across a chasm. This analogy energized the group in the moment and served the purpose of emphasizing the collective in such a way that different speakers referenced the analogy in off-the-cuff ways throughout the meeting. It was so significant that it reappeared at RISC's annual gathering months later. Of course, metaphors and analogies have a shadow side as well. During the yearly gathering, one speaker used the metaphor of being "at war" with a particular issue. While I understand that the speaker's intent was to establish opposition, war is a particularly violent metaphor that entails clear winners and losers. The goal of RISC is not violence, and certainly not an outcome of winners or losers, but rather the mutual flourishing of all. Care is needed with our analogies and metaphors, lest we alienate others, cross purposes with strategic goals, or lead others down a path we do not intend. I would also emphasize the importance of avoiding ableist metaphors that equate injustice with physical disability.

---

9. Technically, these might belong in the section below on rhetoric, but I have included them here to suggest their importance for helping concretize the ideas we are communicating.

Concretizing devices help us deal in the realities of life with listeners, break down complexities or abstractions, help them identify with problems and solutions, and give them a sense of where they fit into the work toward strategic goals. We do well to consider the variety of ways we make public proclamation concrete in service of our collective work. At this point, I would encourage you to pause and take stock of these elements in a previous instance of public proclamation or identify ones that might be helpful as you continue your developmental work.

LIVELY LANGUAGE, EMOTION, AND TONE

As with concretizing devices, the artistry of language and the emotion and tone of public proclamation are ignored at our peril. In Frank Thomas's book *How to Preach a Dangerous Sermon*, he makes the case for "dangerous sermons," or sermons that attend to what Thomas calls the "moral imagination." By moral imagination, Thomas means "the ability of the preacher, intuitive or otherwise, in the midst of the chaotic experiences of human life and existence, to grasp and share God's abiding wisdom and ethical truth in order to benefit the individual and common humanity."[10] One of the four qualities of dangerous sermons—Thomas uses two public speeches as his examples—is "the language of poetry and art that lifts and elevates the human spirit by touching the emotive chords of wonder, mystery, and hope."[11]

Language

Artistry of language is not ornamentation or rhetorical flourish for its own sake, nor for manipulative purposes. Instead, it is integral to communicational design and conveying passion and authenticity in the speaking moment. In my experience, this focus on artistry of language—or, more specifically, rhetoric—is often neglected in the preaching classroom. Perhaps this is because of the long-standing tension between rhetoric and preaching within homiletical circles.[12] Whatever the reason, neglect of classical rhetorical devices often assumes that careful, passionate, compelling, and lively artistic language is "caught rather

---

10. Frank A. Thomas, *How to Preach a Dangerous Sermon* (Abingdon, 2018), xl.
11. Thomas, 20.
12. See, for instance, James F. Kay, *Preaching and Theology* (Chalice, 2008).

than taught." However, savvy speakers carefully learn, consider, and incorporate the artistry of language into public proclamation as avenues for greater memorability, ease of listening, and emotional effect among those who gather. By "carefully," I mean that a speaker will not likely deploy all these devices in an instance of public proclamation; some discernment is needed.

Following are some of the most commonly used rhetorical devices or figures of speech.[13] This list is not exhaustive, but it serves as a jumping-off point for considering the ways that public proclamation can create a communicative moment that is more conducive for listeners. As you read through them, consider what you might have used before or tend to use and what devices might be new and helpful to incorporate.

Slogans

While slogans aren't exactly a classic rhetorical device, they do allow people to distill the message and action into bite-size, memorable, and portable forms. Using slogans helps those who are gathered connect to the new frames being offered, brings strategic goals into view, creates a sense of unity and belonging among those gathered (and among other speakers, if present), and solidifies the central claim. For instance, I have been sharing that when speakers at RISC gatherings say, "Because justice demands," those gathered complete the phrase with "Risk!" Being part of RISC means knowing this phrase: It fosters group identity and reinforces the message that real labor and risk-taking are involved in working for justice. If no slogan exists for the group, cause, or event for which you are speaking, consider how your central statements might help you craft one that is appropriate.

Verbal and Bodily Participation

Closely connected to slogans are encouraging and planning for verbal and bodily participation from the gathered. RISC uses a slogan that invites verbal participation by allowing space for those gathered to fill in the blank with a prescribed word or phrase. For similar reasons as slogans, this is a good idea, helping listeners become more active participants through verbal or bodily participation. If verbal participation is expected

---

13. These devices typically come under the category of style, according to manuals of rhetoric.

after an initial phrase and if participants should fill in the blank, this device is known as "ellipsis." Speakers might consider intentionally teaching a word or phrase and noting when listeners should participate or allowing it to catch on more organically (but still purposefully) through the use of repetition and pause, gesture, and/or facial expression. Speakers can also encourage people's bodily participation through clapping hands, raising hands, standing up, or some combination of words and embodiment.

Repetition

Here we enter more into the territory of classic rhetorical categories. Several forms of repetition can be effective.

Anaphora

Anaphora is the repetition of words or phrases at the *beginning* of a sentence and speech unit. Perhaps the most famous instance of anaphora in contemporary US history is Martin Luther King Jr.'s "I have a dream" phrase, which is repeated at the beginning of speech units at the end of the speech five to seven times, depending on how we might count it.

Epistrophe

Epistrophe is the opposite of anaphora, repeating words or phrases at the *end* of a sentence and speech unit.

Alliteration and Assonance

Alliteration is the repetition of similar consonantal sounds; assonance is the repetition of vowel sounds in adjacent words. For instance, Liz Theoharis uses alliteration when she says, "When a climate crisis is wreaking havoc on the lives and livelihood of people all over this world."[14] Both "climate crisis" and "lives and livelihood" are instances of alliteration. The long "I" sound in "lives and livelihood" would be an instance of assonance.[15]

---

14. Poor People's Campaign, "America Is in a Time of Crisis: Quotes from the Speeches of the Co-chairs of the Poor People's Campaign at Make Good Trouble Rally," accessed October 25, 2024, https://www.poorpeoplescampaign.org/america-is-in-a-time-of-crisis-quotes-from-the-speeches-of-the-co-chairs-of-the-poor-peoples-campaign-at-make-good-trouble-rally/.

15. Poor People's Campaign, "America Is in a Time of Crisis."

Parallelism

Parallelism is simply "a similarity of structure in a pair or series of related words, phrases, or clauses."[16] Notice how Theoharis uses multiple parallelisms in this excerpt from a speech: "We must rally. We must organize. And mobilize. And sit in and stand up. Not just for a day. Not just for a summer. But until all people are housed. Until all people are fed. Until all people earn a living wage. When our voting rights are protected and expanded. All debt is canceled. All air and water is clean. All people are free to thrive, not just barely survive."[17] The structure of the first two sentences is identical: "We must [*verb*]." It continues with two instances of "Not just for a [*noun*]." There are other instances of parallelism in this quote from Theoharis. See if you can identify them. Parallelism helps create rhythm, ease of listening, and memorability in public speaking.

Rhetorical Questions

Rhetorical questions are often-used and well-known devices. Of course, rhetorical questions are not open-ended questions for the audience but are questions intended for the purpose of asserting what the speaker or listeners already know. My caution with rhetorical questions is that they can be overused and in ways that avoid making more declarative and assertive statements. While speakers should be careful of sounding too assertive or demanding, at the same time they should not abdicate their sense of authority—intentionally or unintentionally—through the use of rhetorical questions. I encourage the strategic, pointed use of rhetorical questions to maximize their effect.

Personification

Like analogies, metaphors, and similes, personification helps speakers make vivid comparisons by "investing abstractions or inanimate objects with human qualities or abilities."[18] In addition to making abstractions

---

16. Edward P. J. Corbett and Robert J. Connors, *Classical Rhetoric for the Modern Student* (Oxford University Press, 1999), 381.
17. Poor People's Campaign, "America Is in a Time of Crisis."
18. Corbett and Connors, *Classical Rhetoric for the Modern Student*, 402.

more familiar, personification can heighten the rhetorical force of what we are saying. In planning to use personification, we might try to identify the ideas, values, forces, or structures that work malignantly or positively, then simply find ways to describe them in human terms. For instance, in connection to school underfunding, a speaker might talk about how "our school budget reaches into the pockets of our children's futures and steals from their possibility." In this instance, the school budget and children's futures are personified as a way of communicating the long-term effects of underfunding schools. Few would dream of stealing from children—and even more, reaching into their pockets to steal from them—so the example ramps up the moral seriousness of the issue at hand.

Hyperbole

Closely connected to personification is hyperbole, the "use of exaggerated terms for the purpose of emphasis or heightened effect."[19] One example of this is how William J. Barber II employs Jesus' words in Matthew 25 as a way of emphasizing his incredulity at those who oppose the goals of the Poor People's Campaign: "If our demands are wrong, then someone ought to have the courage to say Jesus was wrong when he said the nations will be judged by the question 'When I was hungry, did you feed me? When I was thirsty, did you give me something to drink? When I was naked, did you clothe me? When I was a stranger, did you welcome me?'"[20] Here Barber suggests how foolish it would be for someone in contemporary times to stand up and tell Jesus that he was wrong. Hyperbole can be particularly effective in characterizing the stances of opposing forces, as well as the potential damage when those forces come together.

"Let Us" and "May We"

One final note in these rhetorical categories. The use of "let us" and "may we" are anaphoric mainstays in speeches. However, I would urge us to be careful of what I call "salad language" (lettuce do this, lettuce do that) in public proclamation. Speakers can often use these phrases at the end of speeches when inviting people into action and

---

19. Corbett and Connors, 403.
20. Poor People's Campaign, "America Is in a Time of Crisis."

response. However, "let us" and "may we" can obscure the invitations to response. Instead, consider if active verbal constructions rather than first-person-plural queries might be much more effective and clear for those who are listening. Consider the following: "Let us put love into action. Let us come together. Let us work for justice." Parallelism provides rhythm here, but the invitation to action is somewhat weakened. Instead, consider this possibility: "The time is now! It is time to turn our love into action. Time to come together. Time to work for justice." You might play with variations of this example to get a feel for what might work for you. As a rule of thumb, ask yourself if "let us" or "may we" softens the invitation to response too much or if active verbs help communicate the urgency and response more effectively.

Conveying Emotion and Tone

Planning for public proclamation should consider the affective dimension as well. As classical rhetoric has acknowledged since Aristotle, *pathos* is a mode of appeal for public speakers. Those who preach know well how preaching connects to human emotions; this is part of considering the whole being of people. Again, we are right to be concerned about manipulation, lest public proclamation transform into nefarious authoritarian speech. This concern should not prevent us from naming the kinds of emotions we experience as speakers, the emotions our listeners might experience, or those emotions we might want to name or evoke through public proclamation. People are not often moved to action simply by the facts of the situation. *Logos* (logical appeal) and *ethos* (the credibility of the speaker) work in tandem with *pathos*, though in different proportions, depending on the listener's values. In situations of public proclamation, most people who are present already care about the issue at hand. Part of what they hope for is that faith leaders share their concerns, fears, hopes, and dreams and can communicate in ways that meet their own emotions or that move them in responsible ways.[21] If opposing viewpoints are present, emotion can help sway people toward another perspective.

Put another way, we should consider the tone of our public proclamation. Here we do not need to reinvent the wheel. If we have carefully crafted a central purpose statement, then we should have some ideas about the kind of emotions that might be evoked and the tone that

---

21. For further discussion as it relates to preaching, see Lucy Lind Hogan and Robert Stephen Reid, *Connecting with the Congregation: Rhetoric and the Art of Preaching* (Abingdon, 1999), 69–88.

we might want to set in public proclamation. What words in your central purpose statements frame emotions and suggest tone? While there might be a range of emotions expressed in a particular instance of public proclamation and while a kind of emotional arc is perhaps invoked, the central purpose statement can be particularly effective in helping us name a primary emotion or the kind of emotion and tone that will be at the close. Recall the list of verbs from chapter 4 as possibilities to be used in central purpose statements for public proclamation:

agitate	foster empathy
build coalitions	inspire
call to account	lament
celebrate	offer comfort
denounce	persuade
disturb	stand in solidarity
encourage	support
energize	unite
engage in critical thinking	witness to
express outrage	

We might distill these words and phrases for the central purpose statement into some core emotional verbs:

—Empathize
—Express anger or outrage
—Lament
—Comfort
—Unify
—Uplift
—Energize
—Celebrate

Acknowledging these emotions helps us strike the right tone and encourages us to discern appropriate concretizing and rhetorical devices and to consider appropriate elements of embodiment. All these factors are important in helping our public proclamation meet the context appropriately and effectively.

Consider one of the central purpose statements offered in chapter 4 with regard to the police murder of Sonya Massey: "The purpose of this public proclamation is to declare God's condemnation of violence in order to persuade the city council to take corrective action on policing." The primary emotion we might associate then is "express anger or outrage." While the second half of the central purpose statement points to persuading the city council, which would certainly be a component of this instance of public proclamation, a speech that expresses outrage and allows those gathered to identify[22] their own outrage together is a responsible, contextually appropriate, and ultimately constructive use of emotion.

Embodiment

As explained earlier, an inherently connected aspect of the how of our speaking is the element of embodiment. When we attend to embodiment, we recognize that the carefully planned language of public proclamation cannot be limited to the words on the page or called forth in the mind. These words must be performed, like a musician performs a musical score.[23] And as we know from music, performative decisions can either complement the score or ruin it. We do well to think about how embodiment works in tandem with our words to create additional, important dynamics for public proclamation. The following elements are worthy of consideration:

Speed/Rate

Consider well how your rate of speaking complements the dynamics of emotion and tone, not just about how speed or rate affects listeners' ability to listen well. Again, go back to the central purpose statement. For example, how does the purpose of lament relate to the rate of speaking versus that of energizing those who have gathered? Typically, lament is slower while energizing is faster.

Cadence

Cadence differs from speed or rate of speaking. Think about the rhythms you create with different elements of public proclamation. While some

---

22. I use the term "identify" intentionally here. For more on identification, see Kenneth Burke, *A Rhetoric of Motives* (University of California Press, 1969).
23. There is a difference between the ideas of "performance" and "performative." Many authors place both terms in a similar, pejorative frame, using both to describe self-directed behaviors in the work of speaking that attempt to point the spotlight on the speaker rather than on the message or the Divine. Along with many homileticians, however, I consider performance to be a neutral term and a matter of fact. With the analogy of the musical score, we can see how public proclamation must somehow take form through multiple aspects of embodiment.

sections might be plainer and more similar to cadences of conversational speech, parts that use different types of repetition or other rhetorical devices might be spoken with cadences that feel more rhythmic and poetic. Intentional variations in cadence, as with speed and rate, can help public proclamation feel dynamic, point toward shifts in different parts of the speech, and signal changes in emotion and energy. Try reading aloud one of the earlier examples, thinking intentionally about cadence.

Volume

While, at a basic level, speakers must be heard, volume can work in a similar fashion as cadence. Lower volumes can signal soberness and seriousness. Louder volumes can be connected to appeals to unity and action. A stage whisper can emphasize something important. Carefully consider how volume plays a role in communicating the content, purpose, and tone of your public proclamation.

Tone of Voice

Volume does not work alone. A louder volume can just as easily communicate anger as joy. In addition to the actual decibels, tone of voice signals what we mean and helps those who have gathered to discern differences in content. Try the following exercise: Practice with your own voice the answer to the following questions. Risk feeling a little silly by simply expressing sound without words or, alternatively, saying the underlined words aloud in a tone that matches it. How does <u>hope</u> sound? How does <u>anger</u> sound? How does <u>unity</u> sound? How does <u>seriousness</u> sound? How does <u>comfort</u> sound? What do you hear when you listen to the sound of your voice? What bodily sensations do you notice in your own body as you embody these tones? For instance, does your face tighten at <u>anger</u>? What relaxes in your body at <u>comfort</u>?

Pause

As speakers, we're sometimes so caught up in communicating the words we write or plan that we fail to account for pause. But—[see what I did here?] there is power in the pause. The pause is a space in which those gathered are invited to participate, even silently, in which their imaginations are activated, and in which they are given space to come to terms with what they are feeling. The pause can communicate our intentions and be the space where the rhetorical force of communication comes alive. Homiletician Evans Crawford is clear about the sacred nature of pause in Black church contexts, calling it "an anticipatory silence, a silence that is heard as well as shared. This heard and shared silence reminds us that preaching is not something that is under the control of the preacher alone; it is a communal event that also involves hearers and others."[24] Consider how pause can be a poignant, pregnant moment for public proclamation.

Posture, Gesture, and Facial Expression

Moving away from the embodiment of voice alone, we do well to account for posture, gesture, and facial expressions. It is a well-worn adage that body language performs a great deal of our communication. I realize that planning or scripting posture, gesture, and facial expression can make us feel inauthentic, overrehearsed, or distant from the speaking moment. In order to avoid this but still be intentional, I would recommend that speakers get a sense of their bodies ahead of time. Again, risk feeling a little silly by practicing with the following exercise what it feels like to communicate through the body. Whether you sit or stand, and within the realm of what is possible in your own body (accounting for disability and mobility challenges), consider the same questions we explored above with regard to tone: How might hope be expressed through your posture, gesture, and facial expression? Now try these: Anger? Unity? Seriousness? Comfort? Feel free to add more. What sensations do you notice in your own body? What words come to mind that accompany your physical expression? What responses and reactions can you imagine anticipating from others as you employ these expressions?

Notes/Manuscript, Eye Contact, and Podiums

There is much debate in homiletical and public speaking circles about using notes and manuscripts while delivering an address. Despite whatever convictions others have for one extreme or the other, I remain convinced that there is no such thing as a greater good between those who use a full manuscript, those who use notes or an outline, and those who speak with no notes at all. What matters is that regardless of what method speakers

---

24. Evans E. Crawford, *The Hum: Call and Response in African American Preaching* (Abingdon, 1995), 31.

choose, they are as prepared and comfortable as possible and as engaged as possible with those who have gathered. Listeners understand that people may need to use notes or a manuscript for public speech. What they often do not tolerate is a speaker who rises simply to read a prepared script with little to no verbal or embodied dynamics, eye contact, and engagement with the listeners. In this case, the manuscript or notes become an obstacle. The problem is not the notes or the manuscript; the problem is that in their use they become an obstacle or distraction. Similarly, groups have little patience for a dynamic speaker who makes significant eye contact but rambles or wanders in their speaking for lack of effective planning.

While not always possible, particularly in emergency situations, practice helps minimize the possibility of notes or manuscripts becoming distractions to more effective communication. In all cases, preparation of the central statements can function as a way of keeping oneself on track both in preparation and in the embodiment of public proclamation.

With respect to podiums, a microphone is likely to be on the podium if there is one on a stage or platform. Use of the microphone should guide how one uses a podium or not, in addition to the need for a place to rest one's manuscript, notes, or other materials.[25] In some cases, amplification might come through only a handheld megaphone. In this case, it is probably better to be untethered or less tethered to notes or a manuscript, unless there is some way or someone to assist you by holding what you need. Additionally, with respect to a megaphone, speakers should show deference to those who are leading the gathering or action. The ability to move about should come as a secondary consideration and then will depend on the occasion and speaker's comfort level.

CONCLUSION

In this chapter, I have tried to point to some (but certainly not all) considerations that can help us attend to concretizing devices, lively language, and embodiment, as well as how they can come together to help public proclamation come alive beyond the ideas and designs we might prepare. As with what we have explored in other chapters, much from preaching translates to the work of public proclamation.

---

25. Remember that amplification is for the hearer, not the speaker. In all cases, if amplification is available, use it for the benefit of participants.

Attention to these dynamics for speaking can help our public proclamation come alive and meet the urgent moments into which we are called to speak. I have offered suggestions throughout the chapter to put some of these principles into practice.

If you still want more practice, now is the time to either analyze a previously prepared instance of public proclamation (and with the case of embodiment, even better if you have it on video) or write out fully the instance of public proclamation you have been working on throughout these chapters. I would also encourage you to find someone who might give you honest, critical, and generative feedback on your public proclamation. Solicit input on a written manuscript and conduct a live practice session in order to receive reflection on embodied dynamics as well.

Conclusion

Migratory Speech for Contentious Times and a Blessing for the Work

In his 2024 Beecher Lectures on preaching, homiletician John McClure made the case that the "Christian congregational sermon" is a distinct genre, but one that "appears to have legs."[1] That is to say, homiletical practices that constitute the Christian congregational sermon as a genre make their way into other kinds of communication and bear markers of the sermon while also ceasing to be one. Thus, on the occasions when a public figure like the Rev. Dr. and US senator Raphael Warnock delivers a passionate, faith-rooted speech in his capacity as a legislator to a public audience, some will exclaim that (or wonder if) they have heard a sermon, not simply because he also bears the status of ordained clergy and an experienced pastor. I am not interested in defending the turf of the sermon in making my distinction between preaching and public proclamation. To do so would be to make power-laden decisions about who can preach, what constitutes preaching, and what counts as a sermon.[2] That said, I do think that differences exist between sermons for congregational Christian worship and the kinds of public proclamation I have described throughout this book.

---

1. John S. McClure, "Beecher Lecture I, 'Critical Homiletics and Analysis of the Congregational Sermon as Genre,'" October 20, 2024, YouTube, https://www.youtube.com/watch?v=wUQU3aI9r2M.

2. My previous work has suggested the problems with boundaries of who can rightly be considered one who preaches. See Richard W. Voelz, *Youthful Preaching: Strengthening the Relationship between Youth, Adults, and Preaching* (Cascade Books, 2016).

What people hear when they experience Warnock or others speak is a type of crossover that, in McClure's words, finds the congregational Christian sermon "migrating" or "having legs" and that arrives in the venue of the public square rather than in the context of Christian worship. The congregational Christian sermon has such recognizability because of its conventions (though varied across time and cultures and complicated by factors like gender), and listeners rightly make this association. In the words of Donyelle McCray, what people experience in the kind of public proclamation I have tried to describe in this book is "the shoreline of homiletics, the place where preaching laps up against other forms of expression."[3]

I have attempted to tease out the migration of such markers and practices so that when we go out into the public square we might better operate as those who seek to offer public proclamation for the public good. For Christian faith leaders, most of whom have had an education and experience in homiletics (whether they serve as pastors, chaplains, nonprofit leaders, community organizers, or something else), making those connections from sermon to public proclamation is not something most of us were taught. As a result, public proclamation can be mystifying or intimidating, yet many of us find ourselves increasingly drawn to the public square as a significant part of our calls to ministry. Chelsea Yarborough makes a case for faith leaders, especially those who have been trained in Christian preaching, to do this work as a type of "agility." She writes,

> Preaching agility is the commitment to new rhetorical muscles, spreading the invitation of justice, hope, peace, and abundant love through practices of proclamation at protests, nonprofits, city council meetings, social media, open mics, and other platforms. As preachers, we are in a changing game. Pastors are invited to preach week after week to a group of listeners with questions, wonderings, and curiosity about what it might mean to live the gospel. Yet, to stay in the pulpit and not go elsewhere limits the parameters of sacred speech. Can God's breathing word not be spoken in new ways and in more places?[4]

---

3. Donyelle C. McCray, *Is It a Sermon? Art, Activism, and Genre Fluidity in African American Preaching* (Westminster John Knox, 2024), 1.

4. Chelsea Brooke Yarborough, "Preaching across Platforms: An Invitation to Preaching Agility," *Working Preacher* (blog), April 16, 2024, https://www.workingpreacher.org/culture/preaching-across-platforms-an-invitation-to-preaching-agility. McCray and Yarborough (see Chelsea Brooke Yarborough, *Proclamation beyond the Pulpit: The Expansive Homiletical Practice of Black Women* [Baylor University Press, 2025]) are both even more expansive than what I have explored in this book. While I have been interested here in a very particular set of contexts and purposes, I agree with McCray's and Yarborough's assessment that we need not limit what might constitute faithful proclamation.

To Yarborough's question, I hope that I have offered a resounding "Yes!" I have tried to make clear the connections between pulpit and public square and to articulate the kinds of practices that can help us in preparing and embodying public proclamation in ways that are careful and considered, even if we are called to speak at a moment's notice. My hope is that this book contributes to our capacity for agility, which means learning how to stretch and activate different muscles for different contexts, drawing on the knowledge and strengths we already have.

Public proclamation is vital work, even (especially!) in an age suspicious of both public speech and faith leaders. I acknowledge that we live in a contentious time in the United States. Christian faith communities are divided along the same lines as the general populace. Vulnerable populations feel threatened. Christian faith is under the spotlight with the public and dangerous surge of white Christian nationalism. Concerned faith leaders are discerning their roles in public life in ways that did not seem true of recent generations. Many will choose to be at the forefront of efforts for justice, healing, and repair and to forge solidarity in local communities as well as national and global landscapes, knowing that faith leaders are important pillars of our communities. In these times, every moment and every word matters, even if news crews do not show up or when those in power seem resistant to change.

Those of you who have been doing this work already know how to continue doing so, and I hope that what is in these pages helps confirm and refine the practices of public proclamation in which you have already been engaged. Some readers, however, are or will be looking for places to start. I note again, as I have elsewhere, that we cannot expect to just show up and begin to speak, especially if we carry significant social privilege with us. Those who do typically inflict harm rather than doing good. If you are looking for places to start, ask yourself, *What am I passionate about?* Know that you cannot tackle everything, so do not be overwhelmed by the enormity of work to be done. I am reminded of the oft-quoted line attributed to James Baldwin: "Not everything that is faced can be changed, but nothing can be changed until it is faced."[5] What is the work that you can face? Where is that work already happening in your community? Who is it that you can stand beside, listen to, learn from, grow with, and labor with—and find your voice? Start there. Use what you've read in this book to practice before you speak and to refine your

---

5. "A Quote by James Baldwin," GoodReads, accessed January 17, 2025, https://www.goodreads.com/quotes/14374-not-everything-that-is-faced-can-be-changed-but-nothing.

voice for public proclamation along the way. You might use this book as a study with colleagues and workshop public proclamation together along the way.

I have tried to include many examples in the book, but there are so many more to be engaged. As you continue with the work of public proclamation, I encourage you to seek out other examples in your community and beyond, then analyze them through the lenses I have offered, just as you might listen to and analyze good sermons to become a better preacher. In this way, we can grow our capacity for effective public proclamation and discover the contributions that each of our voices brings into the public square.

In the book's introduction, I recounted that I served as a pastor before becoming a theological educator. In my role as a seminary professor, though, I feel as if my identity as a pastor hasn't ended. Rather, it has just shifted contexts. I remain a pastor at heart, and I hope that there is some dimension of pastoral leadership to my scholarship and teaching. In that vein, let my final words here offer a blessing:

> Public proclaimer, may the Divine flow in you and through your words that work toward the repair of the world. May you find solidarity, community, inspiration, and energy along the way, in both the victories and the defeats. And may your proclamation participate in the great labor of love found in the heartbeat of the Holy. Amen.

Appendixes

Figure 1 Public Context Worksheet: Wide View

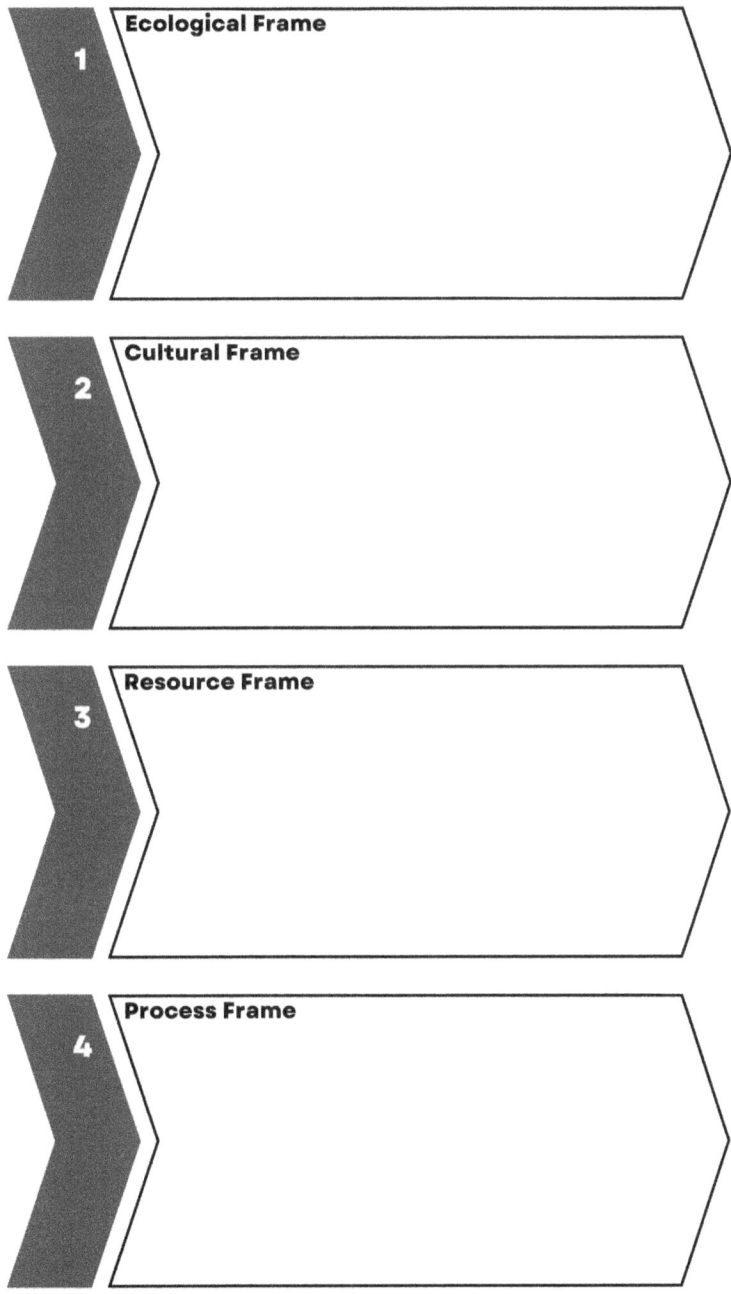

Figure 2 Public Context Worksheet: Close View

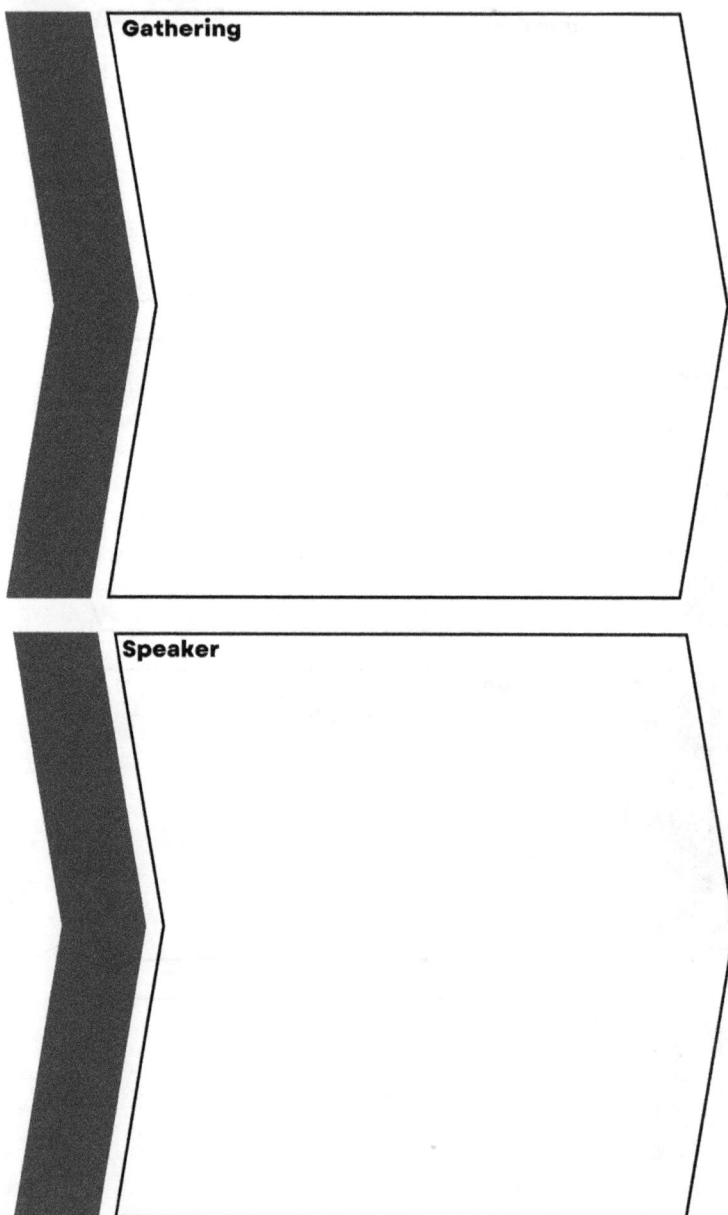

Figure 3 Strategic Goals Worksheet

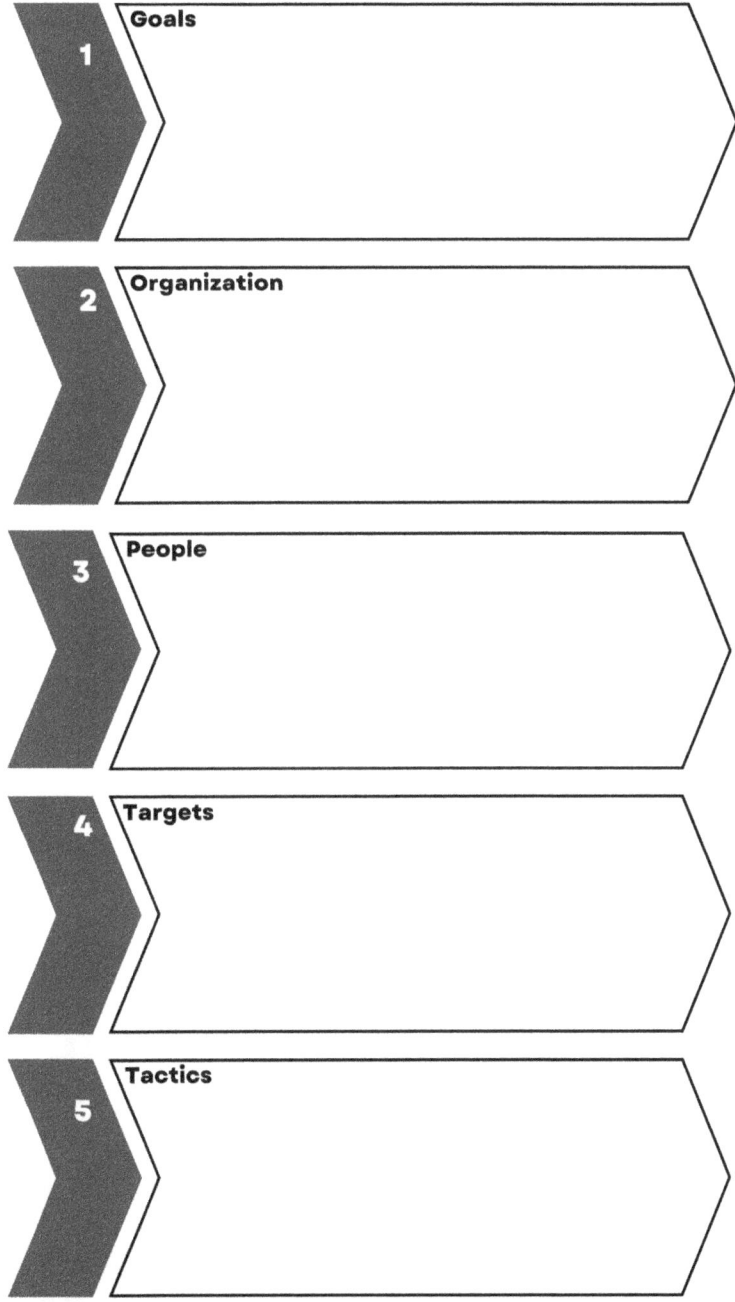

Bibliography

AIDS Foundation Chicago. "Style Guide." June 9, 2020. https://www.aidschicago.org/style-guide/.

Allen, O. Wesley, Jr. *The Homiletic of All Believers: A Conversational Approach to Proclamation and Preaching.* Westminster John Knox, 2005.

Allen, O. Wesley, Jr., John McClure, and Ronald J. Allen, eds. *Under the Oak Tree: The Church as Community of Conversation in a Conflicted and Pluralistic World.* Cascade Books, 2013.

Allen, Ronald J. *You Never Step into the Same Pulpit Twice: Preaching from a Perspective of Process Theology.* Cascade Books, 2022.

Allen, Ronald J., and O. Wesley Allen Jr., *The Sermon without End: A Conversational Approach to Preaching.* Abingdon, 2015.

Ammerman, Nancy, Jackson Carroll, Carl Dudley, and William McKinney, eds. *Studying Congregations: A New Handbook.* Abingdon, 1998.

AP News. "With DUI-Related Ejection from Army, Deputy Who Killed Massey Should Have Raised Flags, Experts Say." July 29, 2024. https://apnews.com/article/massey-911-deputy-shooting-springfield-6ac3ff78bc29f18bd65c6e2763fab96f.

Barber, William J., II, and Barbara Zelter. *Forward Together: A Moral Message for the Nation.* Chalice, 2014.

Blount, Brian K. *Go Preach! Mark's Kingdom Message and the Black Church Today.* Orbis Books, 1998.

Breitenberg, E. Harold, Jr. "What Is Public Theology?" In *Public Theology for a Global Society: Essays in Honor of Max Stackhouse.* Edited by Deirdre King Hainsworth and Scott R. Paeth. Eerdmans, 2009.

Brooks, Kyle E. *Chasing Ghosts: The Politics of Black Religious Leadership.* Georgetown University Press, forthcoming.

Brooks, Kyle E. "Ghostly Ideals: The Hauntology of Black Religious Leadership—Kyle E. Brooks, PhD." USDHumanitiesCenter, February 17, 2023. YouTube. https://www.youtube.com/watch?v=8RTxuQBQxPQ.

Brown, Sally A., and Luke A. Powery. *Ways of the Word: Learning to Preach for Your Time and Place.* Fortress, 2016.

Brueggemann, Walter, and Davis Hankins. *The Prophetic Imagination.* 40th anniversary ed. Fortress, 2018.

Burke, Kenneth. *A Rhetoric of Motives.* University of California Press, 1969.

Buttrick, David. "Proclamation." In *Concise Encyclopedia of Preaching.* Edited by William H. Willimon and Richard Lischer. Westminster John Knox, 1995.

Campbell, Charles L. *The Scandal of the Gospel: Preaching and the Grotesque.* Westminster John Knox, 2021.
Carvalhaes, Cláudio. "Worship, Liturgy and Public Witness." In *A Companion to Public Theology.* Edited by Sebastian Kim and Katie Day. Brill, 2017.
Corbett, Edward P. J., and Robert J. Connors. *Classical Rhetoric for the Modern Student.* 4th ed. Oxford University Press, 1998.
Craddock, Fred B. *Preaching.* Anniversary ed. Abingdon, 2010.
Crawford, Evans E. *The Hum: Call and Response in African American Preaching.* Abingdon, 1995.
Crenshaw, Kimberlé. "Mapping the Margins: Intersectionality, Identity Politics, and Violence against Women of Color." *Stanford Law Review* 43, no. 6 (1991): 1241–99. https://doi.org/10.2307/1229039.
Davis, Avery. "NC State 'Brickyard Preachers' Cause Frustration, Questions among Students, Staff on Campus." *Technician,* October 18, 2021. https://www.technicianonline.com/99039/news/nc-state-brickyard-preachers-cause-frustration-questions-among-students-staff-on-campus/.
Day, Katie, and Sebastian Kim, "Introduction." In *A Companion to Public Theology.* Edited by Sebastian Kim and Katie Day. Brill, 2017.
DeVito, Joseph A. *Human Communication: The Basic Course.* 10th ed. Allyn & Bacon, 2005.
Douglas, Kelly Brown. *Stand Your Ground: Black Bodies and the Justice of God.* Orbis Books, 2015.
Evans, Richard L., *Richard Evans' Quote Book.* Publisher's, 1971.
Farley, Edward. *Practicing Gospel: Unconventional Thoughts on the Church's Ministry.* Westminster John Knox, 2003.
Ganz, Marshall. *People, Power, Change: Organizing for Democratic Renewal.* Oxford University Press, 2024.
Giroux, Henry A. *Teachers as Intellectuals: Toward a Critical Pedagogy of Learning.* Praeger, 1988.
Goffman, Erving. *Strategic Interaction.* University of Pennsylvania Press, 1969.
Habermas, Jürgen. "The Public Sphere." In *Rethinking Popular Culture: Contemporary Perspectives in Cultural Studies.* Edited by Chandra Mukerji and Michael Schudson. University of California Press, 1991.
Hogan, Lucy Lind, and Robert Stephen Reid. *Connecting with the Congregation: Rhetoric and the Art of Preaching.* Abingdon, 1999.
Jacobsen, David Schnasa. "Schola Prophetarum: Prophetic Preaching toward a Public, Prophetic Church." *Homiletic* 34, no. 1 (2009).
Jennings, Willie James. "Speaking Gospel in the Public Arena." In *Preaching Gospel: Essays in Honor of Richard Lischer.* Edited by Charles L. Campbell et al. Cascade Books, 2016.
Johnson, Kimberly. *The Womanist Preacher: Proclaiming Womanist Rhetoric from the Pulpit.* Lexington Books, 2019.

Kay, James F. *Preaching and Theology*. Chalice, 2008.
Kim, Eunjoo Mary. *Christian Preaching and Worship in Multicultural Contexts: A Practical Theological Approach*. Pueblo Books, 2017.
Kim, Eunjoo Mary. *Preaching in an Age of Globalization*. Westminster John Knox, 2010.
King, Martin Luther, Jr. *A Testament of Hope: The Essential Writings and Speeches*. Edited by James M. Washington. Reprint, HarperOne, 2003.
Long, Thomas G. *Preaching from Memory to Hope*. Westminster John Knox, 2009.
Long, Thomas G. *The Witness of Preaching*. 3rd ed. Westminster John Knox, 2016.
Lowry, Eugene L. *The Homiletical Plot: The Sermon as Narrative Art Form*. Exp. ed. Westminster John Knox, 2000.
"The Mass Poor People's & Low-Wage Workers' Assembly & Moral March on Washington D.C. & to the Polls." Poor People's Campaign. June 29, 2024. YouTube. https://www.youtube.com/watch?v=Ilov3Qby5ws.
McBride, Jennifer. *The Church for the World: A Theology of Public Witness*. Reprint, Oxford University Press, 2014.
McClure, John S. "Beecher Lecture I, 'Critical Homiletics and Analysis of the Congregational Sermon as Genre.'" Yale Divinity School, October 24, 2024. YouTube. https://www.youtube.com/watch?v=wUQU3aI9r2M.
McClure, John S. *The Four Codes of Preaching: Rhetorical Strategies*. Westminster John Knox, 2004.
McClure, John S. "The Other Side of Sermon Illustration." *Journal for Preachers* 12, no. 2 (1989): 2–4.
McClure, John S. *Preaching Words: 144 Key Terms in Homiletics*. Westminster John Knox, 2007.
McCray, Donyelle C. *Is It a Sermon? Art, Activism, and Genre Fluidity in African American Preaching*. Westminster John Knox, 2024.
Metz, Johann Baptist. *Faith in History and Society: Toward a Practical Fundamental Theology*. PublishDrive, 2007.
"Minister of Kentucky Church Talks Tornado Damage." December 13, 2021. YouTube. https://www.youtube.com/watch?v=P9B1DyB2lJs.
Molnar, Paul D. "God's Self-Communication in Christ: A Comparison of Thomas F. Torrance and Karl Rahner." *Scottish Journal of Theology* 50, no. 3 (1997): 288–320.
Moss, Otis, III. *Blue Note Preaching in a Post-Soul World: Finding Hope in an Age of Despair*. Westminster John Knox, 2015.
Myers, Jacob D. *Stand-Up Preaching: Homiletical Insights from Contemporary Comedians*. Cascade Books, 2022.
Orbe, Mark P. *Constructing Co-cultural Theory: An Explication of Culture, Power, and Communication*. SAGE, 1997.
Perkins, Miriam Y. (Miriam Yvonne). "The Praxis of Prophetic Voice: Martin Luther King Jr. and Strategies for Resistance." *Black Theology* 17, no. 3 (2019): 241–57. https://doi.org/10.1080/14769948.2019.1688089.

"Poor, Disenfranchised, Clergy and Allies Launch Movement for Moral Revival in America." Repairers of the Breach, December 4, 2017. YouTube. https://www.youtube.com/watch?v=eyRdJjXO4wk.

Poor People's Campaign. "About." Accessed July 24, 2024. https://www.poorpeoplescampaign.org/about/.

Poor People's Campaign. "America Is in a Time of Crisis: Quotes from the Speeches of the Co-chairs of the Poor People's Campaign at Make Good Trouble Rally." Accessed October 25, 2024. https://www.poorpeoplescampaign.org/america-is-in-a-time-of-crisis-quotes-from-the-speeches-of-the-co-chairs-of-the-poor-peoples-campaign-at-make-good-trouble-rally/.

"'A Public Lynching': Justin Jones, Black Tennessee Lawmaker, Responds to Expulsion from State House." Democracy Now!, April 7, 2023. YouTube. https://www.youtube.com/watch?v=XvOoLYI3NOc.

Pyles, Loretta. *Progressive Community Organizing: Transformative Practice in a Globalizing World*. Taylor and Francis, 2021.

"A Quote by James Baldwin." GoodReads. Accessed January 17, 2025. https://www.goodreads.com/quotes/14374-not-everything-that-is-faced-can-be-changed-but-nothing.

RISC. "RISC." Accessed July 15, 2024. https://www.riscrichmond.org/.

"RISC's Response to Mayor Stoney's Rejection of Program." *Richmond Times-Dispatch*, August 29, 2023. YouTube. https://www.youtube.com/watch?v=ySMvtW_FZgM.

Rodríguez, Rubén Rosario, ed., *T&T Clark Handbook of Political Theology*. Bloomsbury, 2019.

Salvatierra, Alexia, and Peter Heltzel. *Faith-Rooted Organizing: Mobilizing the Church in Service to the World*. InterVarsity, 2013.

Saunders, Stanley P., and Charles L. Campbell. *The Word on the Street: Performing the Scriptures in the Urban Context*. Wipf and Stock, 2006.

Schade, Leah D., Jerry L. Sumney, and Emily Askew. *Introduction to Preaching: Scripture, Theology, and Sermon Preparation*. Rowman and Littlefield, 2023.

Sheppard, Phillis-Isabella, Dawn Ottoni-Wilhelm, and Ronald J. Allen, eds. *Preaching Prophetic Care: Building Bridges to Justice*. Pickwick, 2018.

Suchocki, Marjorie Hewitt. *The Whispered Word: A Theology of Preaching*. Chalice, 1999.

"Theological Foundations and Policies and Criteria for the Ordering of Ministry of the Christian Church (Disciples of Christ)." May 8, 2014. https://cdn.disciples.org/wp-content/uploads/2014/07/06162557/TFPCOM-Final.pdf.

Thomas, Frank A. *How to Preach a Dangerous Sermon*. Abingdon, 2018.

Thomas, Frank A. *They Like to Never Quit Praisin' God: The Role of Celebration in Preaching*. Rev. and updated ed. Pilgrim, 2013.

Ting-Toomey, Stella, and Atsuko Kurogi. "Facework Competence in Intercultural Conflict: An Updated Face-Negotiation Theory," *International Journal of Intercultural Relations* 22, no. 2 (1988), 187–225.

Tisdale, Leonora Tubbs. *Preaching as Local Theology and Folk Art*. Fortress, 1997.
Tisdale, Leonora Tubbs, and Thomas H. Troeger. *A Sermon Workbook: Exercises in the Art and Craft of Preaching*. Abingdon, 2013.
Underwood, Beau, and Brian Kaylor. "The Sermon Michael Flynn Hopes You'll Hear." *Word&Way* (blog). July 14, 2022. https://wordandway.org/2022/07/14/the-sermon-michael-flynn-hopes-youll-hear/.
Union Presbyterian Seminary. "Mission & Vision." Accessed January 15, 2025. https://www.upsem.edu/about/mission-vision/.
Voelz, Richard W. *Preaching to Teach: Inspire People to Think and Act*. Abingdon, 2019.
Voelz, Richard W. *Youthful Preaching: Strengthening the Relationship between Youth, Adults, and Preaching*. Cascade Books, 2016.
VPM. "Richmond Clergy Demand Police End Violent Response to Protests." June 30, 2020. https://www.vpm.org/news/2020-06-30/richmond-clergy-demand-police-end-violent-response-to-protests.
Wagner, Kimberly R. *Fractured Ground*. Westminster John Knox, 2023.
Warnock, Raphael G. "Preaching and Prophetic Witness." In *Bonhoeffer and King: Their Legacies and Import for Christian Social Thought*. Edited by Willis Jenkins and Jennifer M. McBride. Fortress, 2010.
Wilson, Paul Scott. *The Four Pages of the Sermon: A Guide to Biblical Preaching*. Rev. and updated ed. Abingdon, 2018.
Yarborough, Chelsea. "Preaching across Platforms: An Invitation to Preaching Agility." *Working Preacher* (blog), April 17, 2024. https://www.workingpreacher.org/culture/preaching-across-platforms-an-invitation-to-preaching-agility.
Yarborough, Chelsea Brooke. *Proclamation beyond the Pulpit: The Expansive Homiletical Practice of Black Women*. Baylor University Press, 2025.

Index

Page numbers in *italics* denote figures.

ableism, 13n, 46, 120
abolition, 46
action, 94, 105–6
   collective, 107, 115–18
   divine, 85, 87
   God's salvific, 5–6, 24–25
   hopeful, 5
   just, 37, 52–53
   meaningful, 11
   "No action, no peace," 37, 53
   prophetic, 28
   putting love into, 126
   theological warrant for, 86–87
   words and, 14
activism, 6n7, 48, 73, 75. *See also* protests; *individual names/group*
"Affordable Housing Trust Fund," 120
African Americans, 26, 44, 46, 102–3
   and Black churches, 3, 10n14, 130
   and Black prophetic testimony, 26-29, 31
   preaching traditions of, 102–3
   and stand-your-ground culture, 27–28
   See also by name; people of color; *specific topics and events*
agency, 19, 107
aggressive practices, 52
agility, 134–35
Alinsky-style organizing, 11
Allen, Ronald J., 42
allies, 36, 45, 47, 53, 55, 71–73, 75–77
   moral, 75
   and naming alliances, 118

alliteration, 123
Ammerman, Nancy, 58–67
analogies, 120
anaphora, 123
Andrews, Dale P., 11n16
angel at the Jabbok, 85
anger, 88, 127–28, 129–30
anthropology
   anthropological claims, 83–84
   and ethnography/adopting an ethnographic lens, 38
anticipatory silence, 129–30
Apostolic Preaching, The (Dodd), 7–8
appropriation, 103n10
art, 103, 121
artistry of language, 17, 98–99, 121–22
Askew, Emily, 83–85, 89–90, 93–94
assertive practices, 52
assonance, 123
assumptions, 3, 11, 13, 115–17
Augustine, 22
authenticity, 17, 80, 107, 121, 130
authoritarian speech, 2–3, 93, 98, 126. *See also* white Christian nationalism
authority, 7, 15–16, 43, 69, 124. *See also* leadership

Baldwin, James, 135
baptism, 41
Barber, William J., II, 3–4, 30, 35–36, 39–40, 45, 47, 65, 125. *See also* Poor People's Campaign
basileia tou Theou, 29–30
Beecher Lectures, 133

behavioral purpose statement, 16, 91–92. *See also* central purpose
"Beyond Vietnam: A Time to Break Silence" (King), 50–52
biblical preaching, 84–85
Black churches, 3, 10n14, 130
  and African American preaching traditions, 102–3
  and Black prophetic testimony, 26–29, 31
Blount, Brian K., 29–30
bodily participation, 122–23
body language, 130. *See also* embodiment of speaking
body of Christ, 26, 84
Bonhoeffer, Dietrich, 20, 24n12
boundaries and boundary-crossing, 20, 22, 29–30, 133n2
boycott (Montgomery bus boycott), 46–47
Breitenberg, E. Harold, Jr., 21–22
"Brickyard Preacher," 1–2
broken speech, 25
Brooks, Kyle E., 4n, 31
Brown, Sally A., 58n5
Brown Douglas, Kelly, 15, 26–29
Brueggemann, Walter, 30
burnout, 43
bus boycott (Montgomery), 46–47
Buttrick, David, 7–8, 29, 106

cadence, 128–29
calling, 3–4, 27, 52, 134. *See also* vocation
Campbell, Charles L., 2, 104, 106
Canada, 65
Carroll, Jackson, 58–67
Carvalhaes, Cláudio, 6n7
cause-effect/effect-cause pattern, 109–10
celebrative design, 101–4
central claim, 16, 88–93
central purpose, 16, 92–98, 104, 108, 126–28
chants, 37, 52–53, 61, 68

charismatic faith leaders, 2–4
charity, 59. *See also* love
cherry tree metaphor, 82
Chipman, Allan, 6n7
Christ. *See* Jesus Christ
Christian Church (Disciples of Christ), 32, 41, 65, 95. *See also* Hord Owens, Terri
Christianity, 3, 52–53, 95
  ecumenical and interfaith solidarity/sharing, 118–19
  and white Christian nationalism, 2–3, 14, 135
  See also denominations; faith traditions; religion; *specific topics, e.g.,* worship
Christian scriptures, 7, 21–22, 39
Christocentric rhetoric, 26
Christo-contextual approach, 24–26
Christology, 25–26
church, 73, 84
  as community of conversation, 42
  as community of faith, 38, 57
  See also ecclesiology; faith communities; *specific topics, e.g.,* worship
civic spaces, 1, 19, 68
civil rights movement/era, 10, 47, 51
claims. *See by description, e.g.,* central claim; theological claims
Clayton, Tim, 21–22
clergy
  roles of, 4, 41, 53
  See also faith leaders
cliches, 84, 104
climate change, 59
climate crisis, 115, 123
climate justice, 5
close view of context (of public proclamation), 68–69, 77
  gathering, 68
  speakers, 68–69
  worksheet, *70, 139*

INDEX

co-cultural theory, 50–53
code switching, 51
Coleman, Don, 76
collaboration, 18, 45, 100n4
collective action, 107, 115–18
comedy, 108
common good, 24, 63, 111
communication, 9–10
  approaches to, 52
  rhetorical-communicative strategies, 16, 97–132
  work of, in community organizing, 115
  See also specific topics and descriptions, e.g., embodiment of speaking
communicative public theology, 15, 23–24, 32, 83, 86
communicative situations, 15–16, 33, 38–39, 42, 46, 51–52, 54–57
  and discerning what to say, 79–96
  faith leader's place in, 35–54
  strategic goal of, 16, 55–77, 92
community
  and community-building, 18
  and community justice, 5
  See also faith communities; *specific topics, e.g.,* disagreements
community organizing, 105–11
  Alinsky-style, 11
  communication in, 115
  faith-rooted, 11, 80
  issue framing and stories, 115–17
  Marshall Ganz and public narrative, 105–11
  work of, 58
  See also by name/group/description, e.g., RISC
comparison-and-contrast pattern, 111
complacency, 94
concretizing devices, 98–99, 113–21, 127, 131
Confederate monuments, 18n

confessional theology, 23
conflict in community, 43, 101. *See also* disagreements
congregations
  and congregational exegesis, 16, 57–58
  culture of, 38–39
  See also church; faith communities
constituents, 71–73
context
  critical, 90–91, 95–96, 100
  public, 56–69 (*see also* close view of context; wide view of context)
core affirmation, 16. *See also* central claim
counterwitness, 87, 94
courage, 29, 53
Covenant School in Nashville, mass shooting at, 36–37, 52–53
COVID-19 pandemic, 6–7
Craddock, Fred B., 106, 114
Crawford, Evans E., 130
credibility, 48, 126
crises, 2–3, 13, 27, 48. *See also by description, e.g.,* climate crisis; mass shootings; natural disasters
critical context, 90–91, 95–96, 100
critical pedagogy, 29
culture
  of a congregation, 38–40
  and cultural code, 114
  and culture frame, 60–62
  See also by description, e.g., stand-your-ground culture; *specific topics, e.g.,* assumptions

dangerous memory of Jesus, 32–33
dangerous sermons, 121
DART network of congregation-based community organizations, 57. *See also* RISC

data, 119–20
deep frames, 115–17, 119
definitions, 120
democracy/democratic principles, 2–4, 36, 86, 106
denominations, 13, 35, 39–41, 53, 65, 69
detail, vivid, 119
devices, concretizing. *See* concretizing devices
Deyerle, Stacy, 81n
dialogue, 45, 49
didache, 7–8
dignity, 50, 110
   African American struggle for, 46
   social, and "facework," 49
disability, 120, 130. *See also* ableism
disagreements, 40, 42–43, 50
discernment, 16, 49, 53, 55, 66, 81, 98, 107, 122, 127, 129, 135
   prophetic, 31
disruption, 6, 9, 27–28
   avoiding, 56
   of deep frames, 115
   mindful response to, 106
diversity, 38–39, 75, 81
   among speakers, 69
Dodd, C. H., 7–8
domain, 10
domestic violence, 5, 15
dominance, 50. *See also* non-dominant standpoints; power
domination, 106
Douglas, Kelly Brown, 15, 26–29
Dudley, Carl, 58–67

ecclesiology, 38–40, 73, 83–84
ecological devastation, 75, 91. *See also* climate crisis; natural disasters
ecological frame, 58–60
economic status, 46–47
ecumenical and interfaith solidarity/sharing, 118–19

Edmund Pettus Bridge march, 49
education, 5, 9, 36, 44, 46–50, 115, 125
   and school segregation, 36
   and school shootings, 36–37
   and school underfunding, 125
   theological/seminary, ix, 17, 18, 36, 113–14, 134, 136
Emancipation Proclamation, 7
embedded theologies, 87
embodiment of speaking, 17, 128–31
   cadence, 128–29
   eye contact, 130–31
   pause, 129–30
   podiums, 130–31
   posture, gesture, and facial expression, 130
   speed/rate, 128
   tone of voice, 129
   use of notes/manuscript, 130–31
   volume, 129
emotion, conveying, 126–28
emotive logic, 102–3
empathy, 3, 12, 94, 127. *See also* kindness; love
encouragement, 31
enslavement/slavery, 24–26, 46
entertaining speech, 108
epistrophe, 123
equality, 13, 110
ethical formation, 114
ethnography/ethnographic lens, 38
ethos (credibility of the speaker), 126
euangelizo ("to preach"), 7
evil, 17, 104
exegesis, 84–85, 89
   congregational, 16, 57–58
exile, 46
eye contact, 130–31

facework, 49–50
facial expression, 130. *See also* embodiment of speaking

faith, ix, 28, 33, 80, 87
  weaponized, 2
  See also Christianity; Judaism; religion
faith-based language/perspectives, 11, 13, 80, 117
faith communities, 5–7, 11, 13–16, 28–29, 37–40, 59, 62, 80–82, 135
  church as, 38, 57
  representing, 39–40
faith leaders, 2–7, 11–18, 20, 71, 75, 80–82, 86, 88, 91, 100–101, 126, 134
  charismatic, 2–4
  role of speaking as, 35–54
  See also by name
faith-rooted language/perspectives, 9, 11–12, 16–17, 40, 69, 79–82, 96, 101, 111, 118, 133
  and faith-rooted organizing, 11, 80
faith traditions, 2, 5, 11, 35, 39–40, 61, 75, 80–81, 91, 109–11, 118–19
  multiple, 81, 100, 119
"family values," 2
Farley, Edward, 5–6
feedback, 132
feminist perspective, 44–53
First Christian Church (Disciples of Christ), 32. *See also* West, Milton
flourishing, 5, 24, 42, 120
Flynn, Michael, 2
focus statement, 16, 89, 93. *See also* central claim
food insecurity, 5
foreshadowing, 116
fragmentary speech, 25
frames
  culture, 60–62
  deep, 115–17, 119
  ecological, 58–60
  offering new, 116
  process, 64–67
  resource, 62–64
Frayed-Edges Form, 105
free church traditions, 41–42
freedom, 19, 110
  God as, 28
  of kindness, 103
freedom song tradition, 61
Friedman, Edwin, 102
function statement, 16, 92. *See also* central purpose
future, 27–28, 33, 117, 125
  and proleptic living, 28
  See also faith; hope; imagination

Galatians, book of, 101
Ganz, Marshall, 105–8
gathering, 68
Genesis, book of, 85
gesture, 130. *See also* embodiment of speaking
Giroux, Henry A., 29
goals, strategic. *See* strategic goals
God
  action of, 85, 87
  as freedom, 28
  image of, 103
  kingdom of, 30
  love for all people, 15, 23, 86, 90–91, 94–95
  moral imagination and, 28–29, 121
  nature of, 83, 85–86
  salvific action of, 5–6, 24–25
  self-communication of, 23
  See also Holy Spirit; Jesus Christ; theology; *specific topics, e.g.,* time
Goffman, Erving, 48–49
gospel, public, 4–6, 8
gospel, Christian, 5
Gospels, the, 29, 87, 125
grace, 93

grief, 62, 88, 105
grotesque gospel/the grotesque, 104, 106
Group Violence Intervention (GVI), 76
gun violence, 36, 53, 76
   and commonsense gun laws, 2, 5, 36, 114
   and stand-your-ground culture, 27–28
   See also mass shootings

Habermas, Jürgen, 10
harm, 2–3, 18, 25, 56, 84, 87, 135
   stories of, 116–17
healing, working toward, 5, 9, 12–14, 59–60, 69, 71, 135
Hebrew Bible, 30–31, 39
Heltzel, Peter, 11–12, 80
Hillel, Rabbi, 107
Holy Spirit, 83, 85, 92–93
Homiletical Plot, The (Lowry), 99–103, 106
homiletics, x, 7–8, 15, 82–83, 102, 104, 134. *See also* sermons
homiletics, helpful forms from, 99–105
   celebrative design, 101–4
   the Lowry Loop, 99–101
   public narrative, 105–11
   and trauma, honest response to, 104–5
honesty/honest response to trauma, 104–5
hope, xi, 1, 105, 121, 126, 129, 134
   faith-rooted, 17
   grounding in, 9–11, 69, 79
   and hopeful action, 5
   "mak[ing] hope public," 26
   and moral imagination, 28–29, 121
   and radical imagination, 30, 33, 110n
   role in prophetic preaching, 11n15
   stories of, 116–17
   the world's (Ganz), 107

Hord Owens, Terri, 75, 86–87, 91, 95.
   See also Christian Church (Disciples of Christ)
housing, 5
   "Affordable Housing Trust Fund," 120
   and housing justice, 115
   mobile home repair-and-replace program, 119
   See also RISC
How to Preach a Dangerous Sermon (Thomas), 121
human history, 29
humility, 18
hurricanes, 48, 59
   Katrina, 87
   See also natural disasters
hyperbole, 103, 125
hypocrisy, 26

identity, x, 9, 20, 40, 53, 60–61, 64–65, 96, 103n10, 118, 128, 136
   group/communal, 46, 48, 61, 64, 122
   and identity markers, 46–48
   moral, 27
   subcultural, 57
"I Have a Dream" speech (King), 110
image of God, 103
imagery, 103, 116–17
imagination
   moral, 28–29, 121
   radical, 29–30, 33, 110n
   See also hope
immigrants, 2
impostor syndrome, 94
incarnation/incarnated *logos*, 23, 26
inductive movement (Fred Craddock), 106
inequality, systemic, 91
informative speech, 108–11
injustice, 115–16, 120
   systemic, 65, 75
instructive speech, 108

integrity, 21, 80
interfaith solidarity/sharing, 118–19
intermediate power, 48–50
intersectionality, 25, 46–47, 91
intervention, theocentric pattern of, 30
Iraq War, 21–22
isolation, 43
Israel (Jacob), 85
Israel, religious caste of, 26
issue-framing, 115–17
"itch," problematic, 99–100

Jackson, Jesse, 3
Jacob (Israel), 85
Jacobsen, David Schnasa, 31, 43
January 6, 2021, attack on US Capitol, 14, 35–36
Jeffries, Robert, 2
Jennings, Willie James, 15, 24–26
Jeremiah, book of, 37
Jesus Christ, 1, 5–7, 11, 23–26, 28–30, 41, 83–85, 87, 114, 125
    action of, 85
    body of, 26, 84
    "dangerous memory of," 32–33
    as God's self-communication, 23
    as incarnation, 23, 26
    nature of, 83, 85
    work of, 83
Jim Crow era, 2
Johnson, Gloria, 36
Johnson, Kimberly, 32n43, 36, 49
Johnson, Lyndon, 49
Jones, Justin, 36–37, 52–53
joy, 88, 103, 129
    and celebrative design, 101–4
Judaism, 30, 39, 107. *See also* faith traditions
judgment, divine, 1
judgment, theological, 86, 94–95
justice, ix, xi, 12–15, 29, 46, 69–71, 75, 79, 90–91, 94–95, 100n4
    just action, 37, 52–53
    and justice fatigue, 94
    peace and/"no justice, no peace," 37, 52–53
    risk and, 61, 122
    work for/working toward, 5, 9, 12–14, 59–60, 69, 71, 115, 126, 135
    work of, 14
    See also social justice, *and by description, e.g.,* community: and community justice; housing: and housing justice

kairotic theocentric approach, 26–29
Katrina, hurricane, 87
kerygma, 7–8
kerysso ("to proclaim" or "to herald"), 7
Kim, Eunjoo Mary, 38n7, 40
kindness, 100–101, 103, 109–10. *See also* empathy; love
King, Martin Luther, Jr., xi, 3–4, 10, 20, 25, 27–29, 36–37, 44, 46–52, 123
    "Beyond Vietnam: A Time to Break Silence" speech, 50–52
    "I Have a Dream" speech, 110
    March on Washington speech, 4
    Montgomery bus boycott, 46–47
    as outsider-within, 46
kingdom of God, 30
Kurogi, Atsuko, 49

labor
    living wage for, 124
    low-wage, 35–36, 46–47
    See also Poor People's Campaign
labor unions, 75
lament, 94–95, 104, 127–28
language
    artistry of, 17, 98–99, 121–22
    faith-based, 11, 13, 80, 117
    faith-rooted (*see* faith-rooted language)

language (*continued*)
  lively, 121–31
  See also by description, e.g.,
    prophets: language of
leadership, 105–6
  public, 108
  work of, 106
  See also authority; faith leaders
learned helplessness, 94
"let us," 125–26
LGBTQIA+ rights/advocacy, 2, 5, 7, 9, 18, 49–50
liberation, 23, 25, 46
Lincoln, Abraham, 7
listening, experience of, 17, 98–99, 108–9, 112
lively language, 121–31
living wage, 124
logos (incarnated), 23
logos (logical appeal), 126
loneliness, 43
Lone Ranger prophet model, 31, 43
Long, Thomas G., 84, 92–93
love, ix, xi, 28, 36, 50, 75, 134, 136
  for God, 65, 86–87, 91, 95
  God's/divine, 15, 23, 86, 90–91, 94–95
  for neighbor, 65, 86–87, 91, 95, 100–101, 111
  put into action, 126
  redemptive self-love, 32
  See also empathy; kindness
Lowry, Eugene L., 99–103, 106, 109–10
  and the Lowry Loop, 99–101
low-wage workers, 35–36, 46–47.
  See also Poor People's Campaign

manipulation, concerns about, 17, 93, 98, 102–3, 121, 126
manuscript, use of, 130–31
March on Washington (1963), 4
marginalized standpoints, 46–48, 86, 90, 111. *See also* intersectionality

Mark, Gospel of, 29
masculinity, performance of, 31.
  See also white Christian nationalism
Massey, Sonya, 86, 90–91, 94–95, 127
mass shootings, 14, 52–53, 88
  at Covenant School in Nashville, Tennessee, 36–37
Matthew, Gospel of, 87, 125
Mayfield, Kentucky, tornadoes in, 32, 62–63, 73
"may we," 125–26
McBride, Jennifer, 21–22, 24n12
McClure, John S., 8, 42–43, 80n1, 84n11, 114–15, 133–34
McCray, Donyelle C., 134
McKinney, William, 58–67
memory
  "dangerous," of Jesus, 32–33
  moral, 27–28
mental health, 86, 91
metaphors, 120
Metz, Johann Baptist, 32–33
mimicry, 103n10
ministry, 4, 39–44, 51, 134
  ordained, 17, 36, 41, 133
  representative, 41
  theologies of, 40–41
  work of, 41, 43
minoritized standpoints, 44, 46–47, 65
mirroring, 51–52
mission, 41, 62
mobile home repair-and-replace program, 119
Montgomery bus boycott, 46–47
Montgomery Improvement Association, 46–47
moral activism, 75
moral allies, 75. *See also* allies
moral authority, 15–16
moral courage, 53
moral fusion movement, 75
moral identity, 27

moral imagination, 28–29, 121
moral memory, 27–28
moral participation, 28
Moss, Otis, III, 19
motivated sequence pattern, 110
music, 61, 68, 102–3, 114, 128
mystery, 5–6, 121
"My Story, Biblical Story, Our (Congregational) Story" design, 106
myths, 28–29, 60

narrative entrenchment, 42
narrative fracture, 104–5
narrative plots, 99–102
nationalism, 75
  white Christian, 2–3, 14, 135
natural disasters, 5, 13, 48, 59, 71, 73, 87, 104. *See also by description, e.g.,* tornadoes
neighbor, love for/kindness to, 65, 86–87, 91, 95, 100–101, 111
New Homiletic period, 106, 114
New Testament, 7–8, 29, 31, 39. *See also* Gospels, the
nonassertive practices, 52
nondominant standpoints, 44–45, 50–52
nonprofits, 4–5, 13, 134
nonviolence, 36, 86, 90–91, 94–95
non-White people/standpoints, 47. *See also* African Americans; people of color
normative preaching, 84–85
notes, use of, 130–31

Old Testament, 30–31, 39
opposition, 42, 44–45, 48, 51–52, 86, 116–18, 120
  identifying, 118
oppression, 29–30, 33, 45–46
  corporate, 6
Orbe, Mark P., 51–52
ordained ministry, 17, 36, 41, 133

organizing, community. *See* community organizing
outsider-within perspective, 46
overwhelm, 94
Owens, Terri Hord. *See* Hord Owens, Terri

parallelism, 124
Parkes, Sam Persons, 83
participation
  moral, 28
  in public proclamation, 41, 99
  verbal and bodily, 122–23
passion, 17, 121, 133, 135
pastoral theology, 88
pathos, 126
pause, sacred nature of, 129–30
peace, 86, 90–91, 94–95, 135
  "No action, no peace," 37, 53
  and justice/"no justice, no peace," 37, 52–53
  See also nonviolence
pedagogy, critical, 29
people of color, 86, 91
  non-White people/standpoints, 47
  See also African Americans
people of God, 11
People, Power, Change: Organizing for Democratic Renewal (Ganz), 106
performance, 128n23
peripheral power, 45, 50–53
Perkins, Miriam Y., 44–53
permission-giving, theological, 88, 105
personification, 124–25
persuasive speech, 108–9, 111
Peters, Kristin, 100n4
Pettus Bridge march, 49
place, 44–53
plots in sermon structure, 106
pluralism, 19, 61, 80–81
podiums, 130–31
poetry, 103, 121

police reform, 91
police violence/brutality, 18n, 86, 90–91, 94–95, 127. *See also* Massey, Sonya
politics, xi, 25, 29–30, 39, 45, 47, 59–60, 63, 82, 109–11
   and authoritarian speech, 2–3, 93, 98, 126
   and democracy/democratic principles, 2–4, 36, 86, 106
   January 6, 2021, attack on US Capitol, 14, 35–36
   and kindness around differences, 95, 111
   and political agendas, 2, 75
   political leaders, 13–14
   and political power, 76
   and the 2024 election cycle, US, 100–101
   and white Christian nationalism, 2–3, 14, 135
Poor People's Campaign, 10, 35–36, 39, 45–47, 57, 61, 65, 86–87
   central/theological claim of, 91, 95
   strategic goals of, 75, 91, 125
   See also Barber, William J., II; Theoharis, Liz
posture, 130
poverty, 75, 91. *See also under* wages
power, 44–53
   collective, for change, 116, 118
   and domination, 106
   intermediate, and strategic interaction, 48–50
   issue framing and, 116
   peripheral, 45, 50–53
   political, 76
   proximal, 45–48
   and resistance to change, 135
   situational, 44
   See also authority; leadership
Powery, Luke A., 58n5
practical theology, 20
   and practical public theology, 23, 32
prayer, 5, 19–20, 63, 68, 76, 93
preaching
   agility in, 134–35
   biblical, 84–85
   normative, 84–85
   prophetic, 10–11, 11n15, 31
   street/"Brickyard," 1–3
   theology of/theology for, 82–83
   See also homiletics; sermons
Preaching to Teach: Inspire People to Think and Act (Voelz), 11n15, 29, 110n
preparation/preparatory work, 16–17, 57, 79, 84, 89, 97
privilege, 18, 47–48, 59, 65, 135
problem-solution pattern, 109
process frame, 64–67
process theology, 32
"proclamation," the term, 6–8
proclamation, public. *See* public proclamation
proleptic living, 28
prophets/the prophetic
   language of, 30–32
   Lone Ranger model of, 31, 43
   and prophetic action, 28
   and prophetic Black testimony, 26–29, 31
   and prophetic care, 11
   and prophetic preaching, 10–11, 11n15, 31
   and prophetic testimony, 26–29, 31
   and prophetic voice, 11, 44
protests, 2, 18n, 36–37, 45, 49, 52–53, 57, 73, 86, 134
   language of, 52
   See also by name/description
"public," the term, 6–8
public gospel, 4–6, 8
public leadership, 108. *See also* faith leaders; leadership
public opinion, 10

INDEX

public proclaimer, three images of
  charismatic faith leader, 2–4
  street preacher, 1–3
  white Christian nationalist, 2–3
public proclamation, ix, 1, 6–7
  central claim of (*see* central claim)
  central purpose of (*see* central purpose)
  context/public context of, 56–69 (*see also* close view of context; wide view of context)
  contexts and relationships in, 39–43
  definition of, 9–14, 79–80
  dynamic, 113–36
  participation in, 41, 99
  preparatory work of, 57
  the self in, 35–54
  shape of (form and design), 97–112 (*see also* homiletics, helpful forms from)
  six fundamental questions for, 15–17
  strategic goals and, 12–14, 69–77, *74, 140*
  strategies for, 44
  the term, 1, 6–7
  theological claims in, 79–88
  theologies for, 19–33
  as vital work, 135
  work of, 4–5, 12, 15, 17–18, 20, 23, 26, 40–43, 53, 55, 57, 80, 118, 131, 135–36
public speaking/discipline of public speaking, 9, 12, 16, 98–99, 107–12, 124, 130
"public sphere" or "public square," ix, xi, 2–10, 13–23, 29–32, 37–39, 53, 55, 69, 76, 79–96, 98, 102–3, 134–36
  the right to speak in, 18
public theology, 88
  communicative, 15, 23–24, 32, 83, 86
  defining, 21–23
  practical, 23, 32
  work of, 21, 23, 32, 86
  See also West, Milton
public witness, 41
  basileia tou Theou, 29–30
  Christo-contextual, 24–26
  kairotic theocentric, 26–29
  theological frames for, 24–32
"pulpit moralism," 31
purpose, 12
  behavioral purpose statement, 16, 91–92
  central, 16, 92–98, 104, 108, 126–28
  See also strategic goals
Pyles, Loretta, 55, 71–72, 115–18

racial justice, 5, 47
racial reconciliation, 11
racism, 13, 49, 75, 91
  and stand your ground culture, 27–28
  See also specific topics, e.g., segregation; enslavement/slavery
radical imagination, 30, 33, 110n
  of the *basileia tou Theou,* 29–30
Rahner, Karl, 23
ReAwaken America Tour (Michael Flynn), 2
reconciliation, 11
redemption, 6, 11, 25, 105
reframing, theological, 28, 43, 87–88, 94, 105
relationships, 39–43. *See also specific topics, e.g.,* disagreements
religion
  ecumenical and interfaith solidarity/sharing, 118–19
  See also Christianity; faith traditions; Judaism
religious nationalism, 75. *See also* white Christian nationalism

INDEX

renewal, 11
repair, 13, 50, 135–36
repetition, 123–26
representative ministry, 41
reproductive rights, 2
resistance, 17, 47–48
   co-cultural, 50–53
   See also nonviolence; protests
resource frame, 62–64
restoration, 11, 59
rhetorical-communicative strategies, 16, 97–132
rhetorical questions, 124
RISC (Richmonders Involved to Strengthen our Communities), 57, 61, 75–76, 117, 119–20, 122
   goal of, 76, 120
risk, 61, 122
ritual, 60–61, 80, 88
role-playing scenarios, 48
rootedness, 81–82

sacrament, 41
"salad language," 125–26
Salvatierra, Alexia, 11–12, 80
salvation, 5–6, 24–25
Saunders, Stanley P., 2
Schade, Leah D., 83–85, 89–90, 93–94
school shootings, 36–37, 52–53
"scratch," solutional, 99–100
"Scriptural code," 84n11
segregation, 36, 47
self, the, 35–54
   in public proclamation, 35–54
   story of, 107
self-directed behaviors, 128n23
self-enhancing (assertive) practices, 52
self-examination, 55
self-love, redemptive, 32
self-promoting (aggressive) practices, 52
seminary, 18, 113–14, 136

sermons
   dangerous, 121
   forms, 17, 97–105
   and plots in sermon structure, 106
   preparation, 16–17, 79, 84, 89, 97
   See also homiletics
Sharpton, Al, 3
silence, 50–52
   anticipatory, 129–30
similes, 120
sin, 26
singing, 61, 68. *See also* music
slogans, 122
social justice, 2, 36, 40–41, 44, 48, 71, 115
social locations, 13, 18, 24, 44–48, 69, 75
social media, 2, 9, 73, 111, 134
social order, 8
social status, 46–47
solidarity, 3, 9, 12–16, 18, 36, 48, 59–60, 69, 79, 94, 107, 115, 118–19, 127, 135–36
speakers, 68–69
speaking
   faith leaders' role of, 35–54
   in the public square, 79–96
   work of, 128n23
   See also embodiment of speaking; language
special needs, individuals with, 5
speed/rate of speaking, 128
spirituality, 11, 19
standpoint theory, 44–48
stand-your-ground culture, 27–28
statistics and data, 119–20
status, social, 46–47. *See also* privilege
status quo, 45, 115–16
Steimle, Edmund, 106
Stoney, Levar, 75–76
stories, 115–17
   of harm, 116–17
   of hope, 116–17

and storytelling, 105–7, 117
and strategy, 107–8
storyboard, 112
"Story of Self, Story of Us, Story of Now" form (Ganz), 107
strategy/strategies
  story and, 107–8
  and strategic interaction, 48–50
  strategy chart, 71–73
strategic goals, 12–14, 69–77
  of a communicative situation, 16, 55–77, 92
  examples of, 73–76
  strategy chart, 71–73
  worksheet for, 74, 140
strawberry plant metaphor, 81–82
street preaching, 1–3
structure-function pattern, 110–11
Studying Congregations (Ammerman, Carroll, Dudley, and McKinney), 58–67
Sumney, Jerry L., 83–85, 89–90, 93–94
symbols, 60–61, 68–69, 80–82, 85, 114
systematic theology, 23, 83

tactics, 55, 71–73
targets, 71–73, 76–77
testimony
  prophetic, 26–29, 31
  See also witness
theocentric pattern of intervention, 30
Theoharis, Liz, 39, 123–24. *See also* Poor People's Campaign
theology, 83, 86
  of preaching/for preaching, 82–83
  See also public theology, *and by description, e.g.,* process theology
theological claims, 79–92, 94, 96, 98, 100, 103–4, 111
  and faith-rooted speech, 79–82
  four types of, 85–88

theological explanation of the situation, 87 (*see also* counterwitness; reframing, theological)
theological judgment, 86
theological permission-giving, 88, 105
theological warrant for action, 86–87
theologies for public proclamation, 19–33
  defining public theology, 21–23
  See also theological claims
theosymbolic code, 80n1
They Like to Never Quit Praisin' God (Thomas), 92–93, 101–4
Thomas, Frank A., 92–93, 106, 110, 121
  and celebrative design, 101–4
Tillich, Paul, 28
time
  God's role in, 28–29
  human history, 29
  See also future; memory
Ting-Toomey, Stella, 49
Tisdale, Leonora Tubbs, 38, 40, 56–57
Tisdale, Leonora Tubbs, 106
tone, conveying, 126–29
tornadoes, 48, 87
  in Mayfield, Kentucky, 32, 62–63, 73
  See also natural disasters
transferable skills, 4–5
transformative intervention, 29–30
trauma, 88, 104–5
Troeger, Thomas H., 106
truth, ix, 35–36, 42–43, 75, 103, 105, 117, 121
  and moral memory, 27–28

United States, xi, 2, 22, 65, 86–87, 91, 135
  January 6, 2021, attack on Capitol, 14, 35–36
  2024 election cycle in, 100–101
  See also specific topics and events

unity, 41, 100, 112, 122, 129–30

values, 11, 39, 43, 50, 80, 115–17, 124–26
   shared, 107–8
verbal and bodily participation, 122–23
verbal formulas, 5
verbs, 7, 93–95, 124, 126–27
   "vigorous," 94
Vietnam War, 51
      "Beyond Vietnam: A Time to Break Silence" (King), 50, 52
violence. *See by description, e.g.,* mass shootings
visual images, 119
visualization, 110
vivid detail, 119
vocation, 3–4, 52. *See also* calling
Voelz, Richard W.
   Preaching to Teach: Inspire People to Think and Act, 11n15, 29, 110n
   Youthful Preaching: Strengthening the Relationship between Youth, Adults, and Preaching, 133n2
volume of speaking, 129
voter suppression, 13
voting rights, 49, 115, 124
vulnerable populations, 111, 135

wages
   a living wage, 124
   low-wage workers, 35–36, 46–47
   See also Poor People's Campaign
Wagner, Kimberly R., 104–5
Walker, Alice, 35
Wallace, George, 49

war, 22
   war economy/militarism, 75
   See also Iraq War; Vietnam War
Warnock, Raphael G., 20, 133–34
West, Milton, 62, 73, 87, 92
   as public theologian, 32
white Christian nationalism, 2–3, 14, 135
wide view of context (of public proclamation), 58–67, 77
   the culture frame, 60–62
   the ecological frame, 58–60
   the process frame, 64–67
   the resource frame, 62–64
   worksheet, *67, 138*
Williams, Ryan, 36–37, 52–53
Wilson, Paul Scott, 83
witness, 12–14, 21, 41
   amid trouble, 9, 12–13, 69, 79
   and counterwitness, 87, 94
   See also public witness
Witness of Preaching, The (Long), 84, 92–93
womanist perspective/theology, 32n43, 36, 49
women's rights, 5
Word of God, 23, 32, 41
worldviews, 2, 42, 114
worship, 80
   Christian, 6–8, 10, 50n34, 133–34
   common, 20, 30, 38, 43
   Jewish, 30
   and worship leaders, 38

Yarborough, Chelsea, 134–35
   Youthful Preaching: Strengthening the Relationship between Youth, Adults, and Preaching (Voelz), 133n2

www.ingramcontent.com/pod-product-compliance
Lightning Source LLC
Chambersburg PA
CBHW020339040925
31982CB00001B/1